First World War
and Army of Occupation
War Diary
France, Belgium and Germany

60 DIVISION
Headquarters, Branches and Services
General Staff
14 June 1916 - 30 November 1916

WO95/3026/2

The Naval & Military Press Ltd
www.nmarchive.com
Published in association with The National Archives

Published by

The Naval & Military Press Ltd

Unit 10 Ridgewood Industrial Park,
Uckfield, East Sussex,
TN22 5QE England
Tel: +44 (0) 1825 749494

www.naval-military-press.com
www.nmarchive.com

This diary has been reprinted in facsimile from the original. Any imperfections are inevitably reproduced and the quality may fall short of modern type and cartographic standards.

© Crown Copyright
Images reproduced by permission of The National Archives, London, England, 2015.

Contents

Document type	Place/Title	Date From	Date To
Heading	WO95/3026/2		
Heading	War Diary of General Staff Branch 60th London Division From 14th June 1916 To 30th June 1916 Volume 1		
War Diary	Sutton Veny	14/06/1916	22/06/1916
War Diary	Havre	23/06/1916	25/06/1916
War Diary	Flers	26/06/1916	28/06/1916
War Diary	Villers Chatel	28/06/1916	30/06/1916
Miscellaneous	App 1		
Miscellaneous	60th Division Training Table		
Heading	War Diary of General Staff Branch, H.Q 60th (London) Division From: 1st July 1916 To : 31st July 1916 Volume II		
War Diary	Villers Chatel	01/07/1916	14/07/1916
War Diary	Hermaville	14/07/1916	31/07/1916
Miscellaneous	Appendix A	06/07/1916	06/07/1916
Operation(al) Order(s)	51st (Highland) Division Operation Order No.61	08/07/1916	08/07/1916
Miscellaneous	Relief Of 152nd Infantry Brigade By 180th Infantry Brigade		
Miscellaneous	Relief Of 153rd Infantry Brigade By 179th Infantry Brigade		
Miscellaneous	Relief Of 154th Infantry Brigade By 181st Infantry Brigade		
Miscellaneous	March Table Issued With Operation Order No.61		
Map	Map		
Miscellaneous	51st (Highland) Division Amendment To Operation Order No.61	09/07/1916	09/07/1916
Miscellaneous	Relief By 179th Infantry Brigade Of 153rd Infantry Brigade		
Miscellaneous	Relief By 180th Infantry Brigade Of 152nd Infantry Brigade		
Miscellaneous	Relief By 181st Infantry Brigade Of 154th Infantry Brigade		
Miscellaneous	Trench Stores	10/07/1916	10/07/1916
Miscellaneous	Amendment, Defence Scheme	11/07/1916	11/07/1916
Miscellaneous	Certified True Copy	14/07/1916	14/07/1916
Operation(al) Order(s)	60th Division Order No.1	10/07/1916	10/07/1916
Miscellaneous	Defence Scheme (Provisional)	00/07/1916	00/07/1916
Miscellaneous	Movements of Troops in Divisional Reserve To Positions Of Assembly		
Miscellaneous	Battle Straggler Posts-Custody Of Prisoners		
Miscellaneous	Appendix "C"		
Miscellaneous	Arrangements for Evacuating Casualties from Front Area	11/07/1916	11/07/1916
Operation(al) Order(s)	G Branch H.Q. 60th Division XVII Corps Order No.16	07/07/1916	07/07/1916
Heading	War Diary of General Staff Branch 60th (London) Division From 1st August 1916 To 31st August 1916 Volume III		
War Diary	Hermaville	01/08/1916	31/08/1916

Heading	War Diary General Staff 60th (London) Division From 1st September 1916 To 30th September 1916		
War Diary	Hermaville	01/09/1916	30/09/1916
Miscellaneous	60th Division Defence Scheme	25/08/1916	25/08/1916
Miscellaneous	Movements of Troops in Divisional Reserve To Positions Of Assembly		
Miscellaneous			
Miscellaneous	Battle Straggler Posts-Custody Of Prisoners Appendix "B"		
Miscellaneous	Defended Localities		
Miscellaneous			
Miscellaneous	Instructions For "S.O.S"	29/09/1916	29/09/1916
Miscellaneous	Support Of XVII Corps By IV Corps		
Miscellaneous	Artillery Co-Operation Support of IV Corps by XVII Corps		
Miscellaneous	Divisional Artillery Support Of IV Corps By XVII Corps		
Miscellaneous	Support Of VI Corps By XVII Corps		
Miscellaneous	Support Of XVII Corps By VI Corps		
Miscellaneous	Heavy Artillery Support of 60th Division by XVII Corps Heavy Artillery		
Miscellaneous	Circular Memorandum No. 4 Hostile Gas Attack	01/08/1916	01/08/1916
Miscellaneous	Arrangements for Evacuating Casualties from Front Area	11/07/1916	11/07/1916
Heading	War Diary General Staff, 60th (London) Division From-1st October 1916 To-31st October 1916		
War Diary	Hermaville	01/10/1916	25/10/1916
War Diary	Houvin Houvigneul	26/10/1916	27/10/1916
War Diary	Frohen Le Grand	28/10/1916	28/10/1916
War Diary	Bernaville	29/10/1916	31/10/1916
Operation(al) Order(s)	60th Division Order No.2	19/10/1916	19/10/1916
Miscellaneous	Relief Of 179 Infantry Brigade By 9th Canadian Infantry Brigade		
Miscellaneous	Relief Of 180 Infantry Brigade By 7th Canadian Infantry Brigade		
Miscellaneous	Relief Of 181st Infantry Brigade By 8th Canadian Infantry Brigade		
Miscellaneous	Table "D"		
Miscellaneous	G.S/392/11	22/10/1916	22/10/1916
Miscellaneous	G.S./392/14	23/10/1916	23/10/1916
Operation(al) Order(s)	60th Division Order No.3	25/10/1916	25/10/1916
Operation(al) Order(s)	60th Division Order No.4	25/10/1916	25/10/1916
Operation(al) Order(s)	60th Division Order No.5	28/10/1916	28/10/1916
Operation(al) Order(s)	60th Division Order No.6	28/10/1916	28/10/1916
Heading	War Diary General Staff Branch-60th Div. H.Q. From 1st Nov 1916 To 30th Nov 1916		
War Diary	Bernaville	01/11/1916	02/11/1916
War Diary	Ailly Le Haut Clocher	03/11/1916	26/11/1916
War Diary	Marseilles	27/11/1916	30/11/1916
Operation(al) Order(s)	60th Division Order No.8	01/11/1916	01/11/1916
Operation(al) Order(s)	60th Division Order No.7	01/11/1916	01/11/1916
Operation(al) Order(s)	60th Division Order No.9	01/11/1916	01/11/1916
Operation(al) Order(s)	60th Division Order No.10	13/11/1916	13/11/1916
Operation(al) Order(s)	60th Division Order No.11	05/11/1916	05/11/1916
Miscellaneous	Table Of Personnel Animals & Vehicles Proceeding On The 16th & 17th Nov.		

Miscellaneous	Programme of Entrainment	16/11/1916	16/11/1916
Miscellaneous	Programme of Entrainment	17/11/1916	17/11/1916
Miscellaneous	Following Amendments to Schedule "A" And Programme of Entrainment 16th Nov. 1916		
Miscellaneous	Appendix "D"	16/11/1916	16/11/1916
Miscellaneous	Table Of Personnel, Animals And Vehicles Proceeding On The 18th And 19th November 1916		
Miscellaneous	Programme Of Entrainment	18/11/1916	18/11/1916
Miscellaneous	Appendix E	18/11/1916	18/11/1916
Miscellaneous	Appendix "E"	18/11/1916	18/11/1916
Miscellaneous	Table Of Personnel, Animals & Vehicles Proceeding On The 20th /21st November 1916	20/11/1916	20/11/1916
Miscellaneous	Programme Of Entrainment	20/11/1916	20/11/1916
Miscellaneous	Appendix F	20/11/1916	20/11/1916
Miscellaneous	Programme Of Entrainment	22/11/1916	22/11/1916
Miscellaneous	Programme Of Entrainment	23/11/1916	23/11/1916
Miscellaneous	Table Of Personnel Animals And Vehicles Proceeding On The 22nd And 23rd November 1916	22/11/1916	22/11/1916
Miscellaneous	Appendix G	21/11/1916	21/11/1916
Miscellaneous	Table Of Personnel Animals And Vehicles Proceeding On The 24th November 1916		
Miscellaneous	Programme Of Entrainment	24/11/1916	24/11/1916
Miscellaneous	Move of The 60th Division Programme For November 25th 1916	22/11/1916	22/11/1916
Miscellaneous	Central Registry		
Miscellaneous	H.Q 17th Corps	15/09/1916	15/09/1916
Miscellaneous	179th Inf. Brigade Report on Raid 10/11 September 1916	11/09/1916	11/09/1916
Miscellaneous	Statement by Lieut B. Peatfield	11/09/1916	11/09/1916
Miscellaneous	Statement By 2nd Lieut. Thompson	11/09/1916	11/09/1916
Map	Map		
Heading	60 Div G.S July 1916		
Miscellaneous	60th Division No. G.S.288	11/09/1916	11/09/1916
Miscellaneous	Report On Raid 10th / 11th September 1916	11/09/1916	11/09/1916
Miscellaneous	Statement by Lieut. B. Peatfield	11/09/1916	11/09/1916
Miscellaneous	Statement By 2nd/Lieut. Thompson	11/09/1916	11/09/1916
Miscellaneous	Central Registry		
Miscellaneous	H.Q 17th Corps	15/09/1916	15/09/1916
Miscellaneous	Report On Raid Carried Out By 2/30th Battn. London Regiment On Night Of 10/11th September 1916	11/09/1916	11/09/1916
Miscellaneous	List Of Booty	11/09/1916	11/09/1916
Miscellaneous			
Miscellaneous	H.Q. XVII Corps	11/09/1916	11/09/1916
Miscellaneous	Report On Raid Carried Out By 2/20th Battn. London Regiment, On Night Of 10th / 11th September 1916	11/09/1916	11/09/1916
Miscellaneous	List Of Booty	11/09/1916	11/09/1916
Miscellaneous	Central Registry		
Miscellaneous	Reference Your G.693, D/-12/10/16	16/10/1916	16/10/1916
Miscellaneous	1st Army	12/10/1916	12/10/1916
Miscellaneous	To Headquarters 60th (London) Division	11/10/1916	11/10/1916
Miscellaneous	From Officer Commanding 2/17th Battalion London Regt	10/10/1916	10/10/1916
Miscellaneous	Telephone Messages Received During The Raid Of 2/17th London Regt		
Miscellaneous	First Army	12/10/1916	12/10/1916
Miscellaneous	To Headquarters 60th (London) Division	11/10/1916	11/10/1916

Miscellaneous	Raiding Operations Night 9th/10th October 1916	10/10/1916	10/10/1916
Miscellaneous	Telephone Messages Received During The Raid Of 2/17th London Regt		
Heading	60th Division 'A' & 'Q' Branch 1914 Dec-1915 Mar 1915 Nov-1915 Dec 1916 May-1916 Nov		

WO 95/3026/2

Secret.

War Diary

of

General Staff Branch, 60th (London) Division.

from 14th June 1916. to 30th June 1916.

(Volume 1.)

Army Form C. 2118

WAR DIARY
or
INTELLIGENCE SUMMARY
(Erase heading not required.)

Instructions regarding War Diaries and Intelligence Summaries are contained in F.S. Regs., Part II. and the Staff Manual respectively. Title Pages will be prepared in manuscript.

Place	Date	Hour	Summary of Events and Information	Remarks and references to Appendices
SUTTON VENY	14th	1.30pm	Orders received that the Division was to commence to move overseas on 21st. Advance parties to leave one to HAVRE on 15th and one to BOULOGNE on 18th.	C.A.S
"	15th	12.30pm	Captain HUME GORE G.S.O.3 left for HAVRE. Unit commenced handing in clothing, & and closing accounts.	C.A.S C.A.S
"	16th		Route marching and musketry continued.	C.A.S
"	16th		Preparations for move continued.	C.A.S
"			Digging, route marching, bombing & musketry continued.	C.A.S
"	17		Preparations for move continued. Digging, route marching, bombing & musketry continued.	C.A.S C.A.S
"	18		Preparations for move continued. Musketry continued.	C.A.S C.A.S
"	19		Preparations for move continued. Musketry completed. Route marching, bombing and digging continued.	C.A.S C.A.S C.A.S
"	20		Preparations for move continued. Bombing completed and all stores expended. Route marching and digging continued.	C.A.S C.A.S C.A.S

1875 Wt. W593/826 1,000,000 4/15 J.B.C. & A. A.D.S.S./Forms/C. 2118.

Army Form C. 2118

WAR DIARY
or
INTELLIGENCE SUMMARY
(Erase heading not required.)

Instructions regarding War Diaries and Intelligence Summaries are contained in F. S. Regs., Part II. and the Staff Manual respectively. Title Pages will be prepared in manuscript.

Place	Date	Hour	Summary of Events and Information	Remarks and references to Appendices
SUTTON VENY	21st		Division in process of movement.	CRS CRB
			Units not moving continuing digging and preparations for move.	CRB
"	22nd		Division in process of movement	CRB CRB
		3.45pm	Divisional H.Q. leave SUTTON VENY, arriving SOUTHAMPTON 6pm and Embarking S.S. PANCRAS. Leave	G.S. G.S.
			SOUTHAMPTON 8.30 p.m.	
HAVRE	23rd	6am	Arrived HAVRE. Divisional H.Q. arrives HAVRE and receive instructions to proceed to rest camp and	G.S.
			troops continue move next day.	G.S.
		10.30am	Divisional H.Q. complete disembarkation.	G.S.
			Division in process of move.	G.S.
"	24th	4.11pm	Divisional H.Q. leave HAVRE.	G.S.
		5pm	Division in process of move.	G.S. G.S.
			XVII Corps orders No 14 received	
"	25th	12.30pm	Divisional H.Q. arrive at St POL. and receive orders to establish H.Q. at FLERS CHATEAU.	G.S.
			Lieut:Col: HUMPHREYS G.S.O.1 and Captain BOLTON G.S.O.2 to proceed to 3rd Army H.Q., H.Q.	G.S.
			17th Corps and H.Q. 51st Division	G.S.
			Division in process of move. 179th Bde H.Q. to PENIN.	G.S.

Army Form C. 2118

WAR DIARY
or
INTELLIGENCE SUMMARY
(Erase heading not required.)

Instructions regarding War Diaries and Intelligence Summaries are contained in F. S. Regs., Part II. and the Staff Manual respectively. Title Pages will be prepared in manuscript.

Place	Date	Hour	Summary of Events and Information	Remarks and references to Appendices
FLERS	26th	7 a.m.	Message received from XVII Corps that Corps Commander wishes to see G.O.C. and Staff Officers 179th Inf. Bde at ECOIVRES at 2.30pm 27th together with C.O.'s Senior Majors Adjutants & Coy Comds of all Bns 179 Inf Bde.	Cpd
"	"	11.15am	Orders received for Divisional H.Q. to	Cpd
"	"	3 pm	Army Commander Lieut. Gen: ALLENBY visited Divl. H.Q.	Cpd
"	"		Orders received to move to Divl. H.Q. to VILLERS CHATEL on 28th.	XVII Corps G.789 Cpd Cpd Cpd
"	"	10 p.m.	Division in process of move. 180th Bde H.Q. arrived at BLANGERMONT. 181st Bde HQ at BUNEVILLE. 51st Division Operation Order No 59 as to training of technical troops received (App 1)	
"	27th		G.O.C. Division visited H.Q. 3rd Army, XVII Corps and 51st Division.	Cpd
"	27th	11.45am	Orders issued for Divisional HQ to move to VILLERS CHATEL at 8am tomorrow. Report Centre to open there at 12 noon	Cpd
"	"	2.30 pm	Corps Commander + B.G.G.S. XVII Corps XVII Corps lecture at ECOIVRES to 179th Inf. Bde Staff + COs, 2nd in Cdrs, Adjutants and Coy Commanders	Cpd
"	"		Division in process of move. 179th Inf Bde HQ ECOIVRES 180th Bde H.Q. PENIN 181st Bde HQ CHELERS	Cpd
"	"	7.30pm	A message sent to 180th & 181st Bdes to say Corps Commander would lecture to Brigade Staffs, COs 2nd in Cdr Adjutants & Coy Comdrs at 11 a.m. on 29th at TINQUES.	Cpd
"	"		2 Battalions from each Infantry Brigade moved up to 51st Divisional Area.	Cpd
"	"	7.45pm	Message sent to Divl. Arty to earmark personnel for maximum T.M. Batteries to go to 3rd Army School on course of 10 days	Cpd

1875 Wt. W593/826 1,000,000 4/15 J.B.C. & A. A.D.S.S./Forms/C. 2118.

WAR DIARY
or
INTELLIGENCE SUMMARY
(Erase heading not required.)

Army Form C. 2118

Place	Date	Hour	Summary of Events and Information	Remarks and references to Appendices
FLERS	28th	8 a.m.	Divisional H.Q. move.	Cnd
"	"	"	300th F.A. Bde took over two gun positions from corresponding number of batteries 38th Div:	Cnd
"	"	8.30 a.m.	Instructions received from 17th Corps that executive orders regarding movements of units attached to 51st Div: will be issued by latter	Cnd
VILLERS CHATEL	"	12 noon	Divisional HQ reported established VILLERS CHATEL.	Cnd
"	"	2.45 p.m.	Orders issued to 179 Inf Bde for personnel for 2 T.M. Battys to be at LIGNY ST FLOCHEL on 30th June.	Cnd
"	"	3.15 p.m.	Orders issued to 180 Inf Bde for 2 companies of same Bn to go to some place near A.C.G. tomorrow for work under C.E. XVII Corps. Div: H.Q. to be informed of Battalion selected.	Cnd
"	"	3.30 p.m.	Orders issued to 181 Inf Bde to send personnel for one T.M. Batty to LIGNY ST FLOCHEL on 30th June.	Cnd
"	"	4 p.m.	180 Inf Bde report 2 companies 2/9th Bn detailed for work under C.E. XVII Corps.	Cnd
"	"	4.10 p.m.	Defence scheme XVII Corps received. Defence scheme XVII Corps type received.	Cnd
"	"	10.55 p.m.	Orders giving detail for work under C.E. XVII Corps received. Division in process of move.	Cnd
"	29th	11 a.m.	Corps Commander + B.G.G.S. XVII Corps lecture to Officers 180 In. + 181st Inf Bde at TINQUES.	Cnd
"	"	12.10 p.m.	Orders issued to G.O.C. Div: Arty, 179, 181 Inf Bdes for personnel to proceed to T.M. School at 9 a.m. tomorrow.	Cnd
"	"	2.20 p.m.	Information sent to G.O.C. 17th Corps + 51st Div: that parties for work under C.E. 17th Corps are detailed from 2/19th Bn. Div: Arty.	Cnd
"	"	4 p.m.	Instructions sent to 180, 181 Inf Bde as to Anti gas lecture by Chemical Adviser 17th Corps tomorrow	Cnd
"	"	4.30 p.m.	Instructions issued to CRE to proceed to 51st Div: to stay there for a week.	Cnd

Army Form C. 2118

WAR DIARY
or
INTELLIGENCE SUMMARY
(Erase heading not required.)

Place	Date	Hour	Summary of Events and Information	Remarks and references to Appendices
VILLERS CHATEL	29th	4.30pm	Instructions received from 51st Div: as regards material + class for rapid wiring to 19th 20th 23rd 24th Inf Bdes	Capt
"	"	4.30pm	Instructions received from 51st Div: as regards Grenade class at AGNIERES.	Capt
"	"	4.35pm	Instructions for party of 2 Corps 2/19th Bn. to commence work 1st/2nd July.	Capt
"	"		Weather fine but dull and cloudy.	Capt
"	30th		Instructions as to training of grenade attachés to 51st Div. received. (Appx. 2)	Capt
"	"	1.15pm	Move of 153 wiring completed. Amendments to programme of grenade training received.	Capt
"	"	3.5pm	180th + 181st Inf Bdes informed of amendments	Capt
"	"	4.30pm	Names for grenade school received from 180 + 181 Inf Bde.	Capt
"	"		G.O.C visited part of the 51st Div line	Capt
"	"		Weather fine.	Capt
"	"		Bde M.G. Corps arrived.	Capt
"	"	11.30pm	Orders received for Bde M.G. Corps training with 51st Div.	Capt

A. ? Captain
General Staff
60th Division
30. 6. 1916.

App. 1.

UNIT.	WHERE ACCOMMODATED	HOW EMPLOYED	UNDER WHOM	DATE WORK TO START
3/3rd Field Co. R.E. less 2 sections.	Right Sector Area (in trenches)	With 1/2nd Field Co. R.E.	154th Infantry Bde.	28th June.
1 section 3/3rd Field Co. R.E.	ECURIE.	ECURIE defences	C.R.E. 51st Div.	28th June.
2 sections 2/4th Field Co. R.E.	Right Sector Area.	Defences of ENTONNOIRS	C.E. XVIIth Corps	29th June.
1 Company Pioneer Bn.	Right Sector Area.	" "	" "	28th June.
1 Platoon " "	Right Sector Area.	"B" Work.	C.R.E. 51st Div.	28th June.
1 section 3/3rd Field Co. R.E.	MAISON BLANCHE.	MAISON BLANCHE defences	C.R.E. 51st Div.	28th June.
2/4th Field Co. R.E. less 2 sections.	Centre Sector Area (in trenches)	With 1/1st Field Co. R.E.	153rd Infantry Bde.	29th June.
1 Platoon Pioneer Bn.	Centre Sector Area.	FORK Redoubt.	C.R.E. 51st Div.	28th June.
1/6th Field Co. R.E. less 2 sections.	Left Sector Area.	With 2/2nd Field Co. R.E.	152nd Infantry Bde.	1st July.
2 sections 1/6th Field Co. R.E.	Left Sector Area.	EMPIRE Work.	C.E. XVIIth Corps.	1st July.
1 Company Pioneer Bn.	Left Sector Area.	Reserve line QUARRIES - Parallel 8.	C.R.E. 51st Div.	28th June.
2 Platoons " "	Left Sector Area.	Support & SOMBART lines	152nd Infantry Bde.	28th June.
2 Platoons " "	Left Sector Area.	EMPIRE Work.	C.E. XVIIth Corps.	28th June.

App. 2

60th DIVISION TRAINING TABLE.

179th Infantry Brigade with 153rd Infantry Brigade.
2/15th and 2/13th London Regiments train in CENTRE 1.
2/14th and 2/16th London Regiments train in CENTRE 2.

DATE	7th B.W.	6th B.W.	5th GORDONS	7th GORDONS	2/15th LONDON REGIMENT.	2/16th LONDON REGIMENT.		2/13th LONDON REGIMENT.	2/14th LONDON REGIMENT.
June 28th	Centre 1	Centre 2	Bde.Res.	MAROEUIL	BRAY HUTS.	ECOIVRES.		X NEUVILLE ST.VAAST	X MAROEUIL & ANZIN
29th	"	"	BRAY HUTS	"	Rt.½ Bn. Indiv.	Lt.½ Bn. Bde.Res	Rt.½ Bn. Indiv.	Lt.½ Bn. Bde.Res	"	"
30th	"	"	"	"	Platoon	"	Platoon	"	"	"
July 1st	"	"	"	"	Company	"	Company	"	"	"
2nd	"	"	"	"	Bde.Res	Indiv.	Bde.Res.	Indiv.	"	"
3rd	"	"	"	"	"	Platoon	"	Platoon	"	"
4th	"	"	"	"	"	Company	"	Company	"	"
5th	MAROEUIL	Bde.Res.	"	"	X Centre 2 Centre 1 NEUVILLE ST.VAAST MAROEUIL & ANZIN				BRAY HUTS	ECOIVRES
6th	Bect Aret.	BRAY HUTS MAROEUIL	"	"	"	"			Rt.½ Bn. Indiv.	Lt.½ Bn. Bde.Res.	Rt.½ Bn. Indiv.	Lt.½ Bn. Bde.Res.
7th	"	"	"	"	"	"			Platoon	Bde.Res.	Platoon	Bde.Res.
8th	"	"	"	"	"	"			Company	Bde.Res.	Company	Bde.Res.
9th	"	"	"	"	"	"			Bde.Res.	Indiv.	Bde.Res.	Indiv.
10th	"	"	"	"	"	"			"	Platoon	"	Platoon
11th	"	"	"	"	"	"			"	Company	"	Company

X Mining Fatigues   Ø Place to be notified later.

App. 2

60th DIVISION TRAINING TABLE.

180th Infantry Brigade with 152nd Infantry Brigade

2/17th and 2/19th London Regiments train in LEFT 1.
2/18th and 2/20th London Regiments train in LEFT 2.

DATE	5th SEA. H.	6th SEA.H.	6th GORDONS	8th A.& S.H.	2/17th LONDON REGIMENT.	2/18th LONDON REGIMENT.	2/19th LONDON REGIMENT.	2/20th LONDON REGIMENT.
June 29th	Left 1.	Left 2	Mt.St.ELOY	Bde.Res.	ACQ	Mt.St.ELOY & ACQ	Back Area	Back Area
30th	Mt.St.ELOY	ACQ	Left 1	Left 2	Rt.½ Bn Indiv. Lt.½ Bn. Bde.Res.	Rt.½ Bn Indiv. Lt.½ Bn. Bde.Res.	"	"
July 1st	Mt.St.ELOY	ACQ	"	"	Platoon "	Platoon "	"	"
2nd	Mt.St.ELOY	ACQ	"	"	Company "	Company "	"	"
3rd	Mt.St.ELOY	ACQ	"	"	Bde.Res Indiv.	Bde.Res Indiv.	"	"
4th	Mt.St.ELOY	Left 2	"	ACQ	" Platoon	" Platoon	"	"
5th	Mt.St.ELOY	"	"	Rear Area	" Company	" Company	ACQ	ACQ & Mt.St.ELOY.
6th	Left 1	"	Mt.St.ELOY	"	ACQ	Mt.St.ELOY & ACQ	Rt.½ Bn Indiv. Lt.½ Bn. Bde.Res.	Rt.½ Bn. Indiv. Lt.½ Bn. Bde.Res.
7th	"	"	Mt.St.ELOY	"	ACQ	Rear Area	"	"
8th	"	"	Mt.St.ELOY	"	ACQ	"	"	"
9th	"	"	Mt.St.ELOY	"	ACQ	"	Bde.Res Indiv.	Bde.Res. Indiv.
10th	"	Mt.St.ELOY	Left 2	"	ACQ	"	" Platoon	" Platoon
11th	"	Mt.St.ELOY	"	"	ACQ	"	" Company	" Company

App. 2

60th DIVISION TRAINING TABLE.

181st Infantry Brigade with 154th Infantry Brigade.

2/21st and 2/23rd London Regiments train in RIGHT 1.
2/22nd and 2/24th London Regiments train in RIGHT 2.

Date.	4th SEA.I.	7th A.&S.H.	9th R.SCOTS	4th GORD.	2/21st LONDON REGIMENT	2/22nd LONDON REGIMENT	2/23rd LONDON REGIMENT	2/24th LONDON REGIMENT
June 30th July 1st	Right 1	Right 2	Bde. Res.	ETRUN	LOUEZ — Lt.½ Bn. Indiv.	MAROEUIL — Lt.½ Bn. Bde.Res.	Back Area	Back Area
2nd	"	"	"	"	Platoon.	"	"	"
3rd	"	"	"	"	Company.	Platoon.	"	"
4th	"	"	"	"	Bde.Res.	Company.	"	"
5th	ETRUN	MAROEUIL	Right 2	Right 1	" Platoon	Bde.Reg. Indiv.	"	"
6th	"	Back Area	"	"	" Company	" Platoon.	LOUEZ	MAROEUIL
7th	"	"	"	"	MAROEUIL Back Area	" Company	Rt.½ Bn. Indiv.	Rt.½ Bn. Bde.Res.
8th	"	"	"	"	Back Area	LOUEZ "	Platoon	Platoon
9th	"	"	"	"	"	"	Company	Company
10th	"	Maroeuil	Right 2	Right 1	"	"	Bde.Res.	Bde.Res. Indiv.
11th	Right 1	Right 2	ETRUN	MAROEUIL	"	"	" Platoon	" Platoon
12th	"	"	"	"	"	"	" Company	" Company

Secret.

War Diary

of

General Staff Branch, H.Q. 60th (London) Division

From: 1st July 1916   To: 31st July 1916.

Volume II

"G" Branch
H.Q. 60th Division
JULY 1916

WAR DIARY
or
INTELLIGENCE SUMMARY
(Erase heading not required.)

Army Form C. 2118

Place	Date	Hour	Summary of Events and Information	Remarks and references to Appendices
VILLERS CHATEL	1st	5a.m.	Orders issued for move of Brigade M.G. Coys up to 51st Div. Area to G to ACQ.	Cpl S
"	"	6 a.m.	Situation report received from 51st Div. No change.	Cpl S
"	"	10.15am	Instructions issued to CRA & 181st Inf Bde about lectures of Chemical Advisor 3rd Army at TINQUES and CHELERS	Cpl A
"	"		& metron	Cpl
"	"	10.40am	Inform Q branch of back for transport for platoons to come to AGNIGNAB to do consolidation confro	
"	"		Ask Cpl	
"	"	11.5am	Report received of the operations Third & Fourth Armies	Cpl
"	"		Brigade Machine Gun Companies move to ACQ during the morning	Cpl
"	"	3.15pm	Further news of operations Third & Fourth Armies received.	Cpl
"	"	4.45pm	Further news received of operations 3rd & 4th Armies.	Cpl
"	"	5.35pm	Situation report from 51st Div. No change	Cpl
"	"	6.20pm	Further news received of operations 3rd & 4th Armies	Cpl
"	"	7.55pm	Further news received of operations 3rd & 4th Armies.	Cpl
"	"	9.25pm	News of operations forwarded to units of Division	Cpl S
"	"	10.50pm	News of French progress in their operations	Cpl S
"	"		Fine day. Sound of guns in the south heard most of the day but most intense from 7am - 11 am and from 2 - 4 pm & then again from 9pm onwards.	Cpl S
"	2nd	1.10am	Situation report received giving details of progress of third & fourth Armies and of the French.	Cpl S
"	"	6 a.m.	News passed on to W Bdes.	

WAR DIARY
or
INTELLIGENCE SUMMARY
(Erase heading not required.)

Army Form C. 2118

Place	Date	Hour	Summary of Events and Information	Remarks and references to Appendices
VILLERS CHATEL	2nd	6.5 am	Situation report 51st Divn received.	Cmd
"	"	11.52 am	Report of raid by 2nd Division received from 17th Corps.	Cmd
"	"	12.12 pm	Situation report received from 17th Corps giving further news of progress 3rd & 4th French Armies	Cmd
"	"	12.40 pm	Further report received from Advanced G.H.Q. of operations via 17th Corps	Cmd
"	"	2.30 pm	Further report received from Advanced G.H.Q. of operations via 17th Corps	Cmd
"	"	5.36 pm	Situation report 51st Divn received.	Cmd
"	"	6.35 pm	Situation report of 4th Army received from 17th Corps	Cmd
"	"	9.10 pm	News passed to Inf. Bdes.	Cmd
"	"		Fine day. Gun fire intense from the South during most of the day. Division continued training with 51st Divn.	Cmd
"	3rd	12.20 am	Message from General SIR DOUGLAS HAIG to troops received	Cmd
"	"	12.2 am	Situation report Fourth Army front received.	Cmd
"	"	5.48 am	Situation report 51st Divn received. Normal situation except for a mine exploded on left.	Cmd
"	"	12.52 pm	1420 186 & 182nd Inf. Bde informed of issue of 1000 skills grenades for training purposes.	Cmd
"	"	5.30 pm	Situation report 51st Divn received. Unchanged	Cmd
"	"	5.42 pm	Situation report Fourth Army received.	Cmd
"	"	7.35 pm	News passed on to Inf Bdes.	Cmd
"	"		Division continued training with 51st Divn. Very little gun fire heard during day.	Cmd

Army Form C. 2118

WAR DIARY
or
INTELLIGENCE SUMMARY

(Erase heading not required.)

Instructions regarding War Diaries and Intelligence Summaries are contained in F.S. Regs. Part II. and the Staff Manual respectively. Title Pages will be prepared in manuscript.

Place	Date	Hour	Summary of Events and Information	Remarks and references to Appendices
VILLERS CHATEL	4th	6.36 a.m.	Situation reported normal in 51st Division area.	Cnl
"	"	12.25 p.m.	Situation report received from G 17th Corps giving news of Fourth Army.	Cnl
"	"	12.56 p.m.	News faxed to Bdes.	Cnl
"	"	5.33 p.m.	Situation reported unchanged in 51st Division.	Cnl
"	"	11.30 p.m.	Seventeenth Corps report progress situation of Fourth Army. Weather fine with thunderstorms in afternoon. Division continues training with 61st Division	Cnl / Cnl
"	5th	5.20 a.m.	Situation reported quiet 51st Div.	Cnl
"	"	12 noon	Situation report Fourth Army received from 17th Corps.	Cnl
"	"	5.19 p.m.	Situation reported unchanged 51st Div	Cnl / Cnl
"	"	5.55 p.m.	News of Fourth Army sent to Inf Bdes.	Cnl
"	"	7 p.m.	Bdes informed that 17th Corps have ordered no restrictions at present for movement in daylight into MAROEUIL and LOUEZ.	Cnl
"	"		Weather wet & heavy rainstorms. Division continues training with 61st Division	Cnl
"	6th	5.25 a.m.	Situation reported unchanged in 51st Div area.	Cnl
"	"	5.55 p.m.	Situation reported unchanged in 51st Div area. Weather fine but dull. Division continued training with 51st Division	Cnl / Cnl
"	"	9.20 p.m.	Orders received from 17th Corps that the Division will take over the line from 51st Division relief to be complete by 6am. 14th inst. (App. A)	Cnl App. A

WAR DIARY
or
INTELLIGENCE SUMMARY

(Erase heading not required.)

Army Form C. 2118

Instructions regarding War Diaries and Intelligence Summaries are contained in F. S. Regs., Part II. and the Staff Manual respectively. Title Pages will be prepared in manuscript.

Place	Date	Hour	Summary of Events and Information	Remarks and references to Appendices
VILLERS CHATEL	7th	5.30am	Situation reported unchanged in 51st Div. area.	Cmd
"	"	9.25am	Order No 16 17th Corps as to relief of trenches received. (App: B)	Cmd App.B
"	"	10.30am	All Adm M G Co Commanders ordered to meet G.O.C at ECOIVRES at 12.30pm q'ai mst.	Cmd
"	"	10.47am	Situation of Fourth Army operations reported by 17th Corps.	Cmd
"	"	5.15pm	Situation of Fourth Army operations reported by 17th Corps.	Cmd
"	"	5.25pm	Situation reported unchanged in 51st Div area. Division continued training with 51st Div. Weather wet.	Cmd
"	8th	5.25am	Situation reported unchanged in 51st Div. area.	Cmd
"	"	5.25pm	Situation reported unchanged in 51st Div. area. Division continued training with 51st Div. Weather fine.	Cmd
"	9th	5.39am	Situation reported unchanged in 51st Div. area.	Cmd
"	"	9.45am	Operation Order No 61 of 51st Div. as to relief of trenches received (App: C)	Cmd App C
"	"	10.47am	Situation report of Fourth Army received by 17th Corps.	Cmd
"	"	5.55pm	Situation report from 51st Div. 51st Div area received.	Cmd
"	"	6.5pm	Amendment to Operation Order No G1 received (App. D)	Cmd App. D
"	10th	5.55am	Weather fine. Division continued training with 51st Div. Continuous roar of guns heard.	Cmd
"	"	11.26am	Situation reported unchanged in 51st Div area.	Cmd
"	"	12.25pm	Situation report of Fourth + Reserve Armies sent by 17th Corps. Fourth Army news sent to Inf Bdes.	Cmd

WAR DIARY
or
INTELLIGENCE SUMMARY

Army Form C. 2118

(Erase heading not required.)

Instructions regarding War Diaries and Intelligence Summaries are contained in F.S. Regs., Part II. and the Staff Manual respectively. Title Pages will be prepared in manuscript.

Place	Date	Hour	Summary of Events and Information	Remarks and references to Appendices
VILLERS CHATEL	10th	5.37pm	Situation reported unchanged by 51st Div area	Capt
"	"	9 pm	Weather fine. Division continued training with 51st Division	Capt (App E)
"	"		Operation Order 60th Division Order No 1 issued to all units. Copy No 19. (App: E)	Capt
"	11th	5.30am	Situation reported unchanged by in 51st Div area.	Capt / Capt
"	"	12.18pm	17th Corps report situation Fourth Army	Capt
"	"	4.34pm	News of Fourth Army operations sent out to Bde.	Capt
"	"	5.24pm	Situation reported unchanged in 51st Div area	Capt
"	"	9pm	Weather fine. Division continued training with 51st Division	Capt
"	12th	5.50am	Situation unchanged in 51st Div. area	Capt
"	"	10.55am	17th Corps report situation Fourth Army.	Capt
"	"	5.15pm	Situation reported unchanged in 51st Div area	Capt
"	"	11.45pm	17th Corps report situation Fourth Army. Division continued training with 51st Division	Capt
"	"		Weather fine, some rain in the evening.	Capt
"	13th	6am	Situation reported unchanged in 51st Div area.	Capt
"	"	10.50am	17th Corps report situation Fourth Army.	Capt
"	"	5.42pm	Situation reported unchanged in 51st Div area.	Capt
"	"	7.0pm	180th Bde report 2/19th Bn Lond R commenced relief at 6pm. No casualties	Capt
"	"	8.30pm	180th Bde report H.Q. established Mont St Eloy.	Capt
"	"	9.0pm	180th Bde report 2/19th Bn relief complete	Capt
"	"	9.45am	179th Inf Bde report relief complete. No casualties	Capt
"	"	11.30pm	17th Corps report situation of Fourth Army.	Capt

Army Form C. 2118

WAR DIARY
or
INTELLIGENCE SUMMARY
(Erase heading not required.)

Instructions regarding War Diaries and Intelligence Summaries are contained in F. S. Regs., Part II. and the Staff Manual respectively. Title Pages will be prepared in manuscript.

Place	Date	Hour	Summary of Events and Information	Remarks and references to Appendices
VILLERS CHATEL	13th	11.51pm	180th Inf Bde report 2/17th Bn Lond R at Cambrigny relief 10.45pm. No casualties. Weather fine. Division completes training with 51st Div. and commences relief.	ap.8
VILLERS CHATEL	14th	12.35am	180th Inf Bde report relief completed. No casualties.	Gd
		4.37am	181st Inf Bde report situation normal. Some activity of hostile trench mortars & artillery on evening of 13th	Gd
		5.7am	17th Inf Bde report situation normal	Gd
		5.53am	180th Inf Bde report situation normal. Two raids attempted failed french enemy's trenches.	Gd
		6.11am	14th Division on right report situation normal.	Gd
HERMAVILLE		10.22am	51st Div HQ reports established at HERMAVILLE to 17th Corps.	Gd
		10.43am	17th Corps report Fourth Army captured BAZENTIN LE PETIT, BAZENTIN LE GRAND and LONGUEVAL	Gd
		1.18pm	180th Inf Bde ordered to occupy post on CHAISSEY Crater and work to be commenced tonight.	Gd (App F)
		1.30pm	17th Corps order relief of all the artillery 51st Div by 6th Divisional Artillery tonight (App F)	Gd
		3.53am	17th Corps order all officers + men of 51st Div left behind in Divisional area to rejoin their Div. by 6am tomorrow morning.	Fd
		4.18pm	17th Corps order Division to arrange for carrying parties for mining work to relieve 2.Bns. 51st Div.	CRE
		4.40pm	17th Corps order Division to take over Sniping School at once.	CRS
		4.45pm	Division passes orders to the Brigade about relief of units 51st Div.	Gd
		5.12pm	Division reports situation unchanged to 17th Corps, 51st Div, 14th + 2nd Divisions. Very quiet on whole front.	Gd
		6.57pm	181st Bde ordered by Division to take trey line as far as VICTOIRE AVENUE inclusive.	Gd
		6.20pm	180th Bde ordered by Division to send Officer to take over Sniper School. 51st Div. informed.	Gd
		11.53pm	Division reports to 17th Corps that small airship passed over Div HQ at 11.30pm in a N.W direction, that wind flying low had was unable to distinguish nationality.	Gd

Army Form C. 2118

WAR DIARY
or
INTELLIGENCE SUMMARY

(Erase heading not required.)

Instructions regarding War Diaries and Intelligence Summaries are contained in F.S. Regs., Part II. and the Staff Manual respectively. Title Pages will be prepared in manuscript.

Place	Date	Hour	Summary of Events and Information	Remarks and references to Appendices
HERMAVILLE	15th	4.50 a.m.	Divisional Artillery report relief complete.	Appx
"	"	4.55 a.m.	Division report to 17th Corps situation normal & same T.M. activity in Centre sector.	Appx
"	"	10.30 a.m.	Coordinates of gun positions Divisional Artillery forwarded to the 17th Corps.	Appx
"	"	12.53 p.m.	Situation of Front Line Reserve Armies reported by 17th Corps.	Appx
"	"	4.52 p.m.	Division report situation unchanged. Greatly increased activity hostile artillery right sector.	Appx
"	"		Weather fine.	Appx
"	16th	12.17 a.m.	17th Corps report situation Fourth Army.	Appx
"	"	4.27 a.m.	Division reports situation normal.	Appx
"	"	10.55 a.m.	17th Corps send further report from Advr. G.H.Q. as to situation Fourth Army.	Appx
"	"	4.45 p.m.	Division reports situation normal. Quiet day.	Appx
"	"		Weather wet. Wind W.N.W.	Appx
"	17th	4.50 a.m.	Division reports situation normal. Quiet night except for an hours T.M. activity about midnight.	Appx
"	"	4.58 p.m.	Division reports situation quiet.	Appx
"	"	7.40 p.m.	Divisional wires G.O.C.'s congratulations to 2/22nd London R. for having killed & brought in a German, thus gaining valuable information.	Appx
"	"		Weather wet with heavy rain in the afternoon & evening.	Appx
"	18th	5 a.m.	Division report situation normal.	Appx
"	"	4.32 p.m.	Division report situation normal. Right sector retaliation given twice for hostile T.Ms. 15 N. by evening. Weather dull, low clouds, fine in the evening.	Appx
"	"		Wind N.E. early morning changing to N. by evening.	Appx
"	19th	4.55 a.m.	Division report situation normal, nothing to report	Appx
"	"	8.55 a.m.	Wind report NE 3 miles p.h.	Appx
"	"	4.58 p.m.	Division report situation normal; quiet day weather fine.	Appx

1875 Wt. W593/826 1,000,000 4/15 J.B.C. & A. A.D.S.S./Forms/C.2118.

Army Form C. 2118

WAR DIARY
or
INTELLIGENCE SUMMARY
(Erase heading not required.)

Instructions regarding War Diaries and Intelligence Summaries are contained in F.S. Regs., Part II. and the Staff Manual respectively. Title Pages will be prepared in manuscript.

Place	Date	Hour	Summary of Events and Information	Remarks and references to Appendices
HERMAVILLE	20th	5 a.m.	Division report continued T.M. activity during night; otherwise quiet.	C/E
"	"	3.15pm	Conference at AUX RIETZ with representatives of Infantry Cavalry Division and fatigues.	C/E
"	"	4.15pm	"O" & "O" Heavy Artillery assisted by Div. Artillery carried out ½ hour bombardment on enemy lines opposite centre sector.	C/E
"	"	4.50pm	Division report situation unchanged and very quiet.	C/E
"	"	"	Weather fine. warm with N.W. wind.	C/E
"	21st	4.50am	Division report situation normal.	C/E
"	"	4.55pm	Division report situation unchanged. Enemy trench mortars active on Right and 5.9" gun shelling left group.	C/E
"	"	"	Our heavy artillery replied.	C/E
"	"	"	Weather fine. Wind N.E.	C/E
"	22nd	4.50am	Division report situation normal. No hostile T.M. activity but our guns & machine guns active in right sector.	C/E
"	"	5.10pm	Division report situation unchanged. T.M.s very active since noon in centre sector. Hostile artillery active in left sector.	C/E
"	"	"	Weather finer. Wind N.E.	C/E
"	23rd	4.45am	Division report situation normal.	C/E
"	"	4.55pm	Division report situation unchanged. Our ½ artillery and Corps Heavy Artillery bombarded enemy on both sides of LILLERS road.	C/E
"	"	"	Weather fine. Wind N.E. Slight.	C/E
"	"	11.15pm	G.O.C. approves of proposals of 180th Inf. Bde to blow two mines in Left sector.	C/E
"	24th	4.45am	Division report situation unchanged. Several patrols went out. Heavy hostile bombardment from 9.15 pm till 11 pm on our right N. of ARRAS.	C/E
"	"	4.55pm	Division report situation unchanged, very quiet day with intermittent shelling on right sector.	C/E
"	"	"	Weather fine. Wind N. slight.	C/E
"	25th	5 a.m.	Division report situation normal.	C/E
"	"	4.55pm	Division report situation unchanged. Very quiet day.	C/E
"	"	"	Weather fine. Wind S.W.	C/E

Army Form C. 2118

WAR DIARY
or
INTELLIGENCE SUMMARY
(Erase heading not required.)

Instructions regarding War Diaries and Intelligence Summaries are contained in F. S. Regs., Part II. and the Staff Manual respectively. Title Pages will be prepared in manuscript.

Place	Date	Hour	Summary of Events and Information	Remarks and references to Appendices
HERMAVILLE	26th	5.15 a.m.	Division report right and centre sectors situation normal. Left sector enemy exploded small mine 30 yards N of GRANGE crater and 50 yards from T line at 2.15 a.m. Orders given to consolidate.	CRA
"	"	4.54 p.m.	Division report situation unchanged. Quiet day.	CRA
"	"		Arrangements made by 180th Inf Bde with 172nd Tunnelling Coy R.E. to blow mine half-way between BIRKIN and GRANGE craters at 9 p.m. Mine exploded at 9.13 p.m. Artillery opened 9.14 p.m. and on (?) formed larger than expected.	CRA
"	"		Weather fine. Slight wind N.E.	CRA
"	"	11.55 p.m.	17th Corps inform Division that British airship will be taking short trip tonight and information passed to Bdes.	CRA
"	27th	5 a.m.	Division report mine exploded by us on left subsector 9.13 p.m. last night. Crater larger than expected. Situation not yet clear but separate report being sent. Quiet night on remainder front. Consolidation commenced the near lip of new crater is held by us.	CRA
"	"	4.55 p.m.	Division report situation quiet the near lip of new crater is held by us.	CRA
"	"		Weather fine. Wind N.E.	CRA
"	28th	4.55 a.m.	Division report situation normal.	CRA
"	"	4.55 a.m.	180th Inf Bde	CRA
"	"	7.35 a.m.	180th Inf Bde report situation on new crater satisfactory and consolidation believed complete.	CRA
"	"	4.45 p.m.	Division report situation unchanged. Enemy trench Mortars active for ½ hour about midday. N.E. Crater situation satisfactory.	CRA
"	"		No casualties. Fine wind N.E.	CRA
"	29th	12.45 a.m.	Division report enemy blew mine 10.10 p.m. on left sector between DEVON and damaged French trench tonight. Observation line undamaged. No casualties reported. T.M.s Barrage was opened by enemy but situation unchanged. Two parties and Lewis guns sent to consolidate position.	CRA
"	"	5.11 a.m.	Division report situation normal on right and centre sectors. We are in possession of near lip new crater and consolidation is progressing favourably. Work on TIDZA (new crater night 27/28th) in [ ] by working party but continued slowly.	CRA

WAR DIARY
or
INTELLIGENCE SUMMARY

Army Form C. 2118

Place	Date	Hour	Summary of Events and Information	Remarks and references to Appendices
HERMAVILLE	29th	6.15 am	179th Inf. Bde. report 2 prisoners captured by 2/15th Bn. Lond. R.	Gnd
"	"	6.40 am	Division inform 17th Corps of capture of prisoners.	Gnd
"	"	8.37 am	G.O.C. congratulates 2/15th Lond. R. on their enterprise.	Gnd
"	"	5.2 pm	Division report situation very quiet. Hostile aeroplane over centre at 2.15 pm. Consolidation of TIDZA and new craters proceeding satisfactorily.	Gnd
"	"		Weather fine, very hot. Slight wind N.	A16
"	"	5 pm	Bombardment of German front trenches opposite centre right by Div. Arty. T. Mortars assisted by Corps Heavy Artillery. Enemy retaliation feeble.	Gnd
"	"		Hostile trenches A16 considerably damaged by 150lb days bombardment. Serves	Gnd
"	30th	5 am	Division report situation quiet. Patrols sent out during night.	Gnd
"	"	5.10 pm	Division report that at 10.15 am. Enemy attempted an attack from behind DUFFIELD CRATER in left sector 2 under cover of rifle grenades and minenwerfer. S.O.S. was sent to Artillery and enemy retired. Situation otherwise normal.	Gnd
"	"		Weather fine very hot. Very slight wind N.E ranging to N.W.	
"	31st	4.45 am	Division report situation normal. In left sector consolidation of TIDZA and DEVON craters continued without interruption.	Gnd
"	"	4.45 pm	Division report situation quiet. CHASSERY crater bombarded by our T.M. and howitzers at 11.5 am with good results. Hostile T.M. active on Right 1 subsector. Weather fine, very hot. Very slight wind N.E to N.	Gnd
"	"		Copy of (Provisional) Divisional Defence Scheme issued this month is attached (App. G)	Gnd App. G.

July 31st 1916

C.P. Ballon Captain
G.S.
60th Division

CERTIFIED TRUE COPY.   Appendix A.

SECRET.

51st Division.
60th Division.   G.32   6/7/16.

    Relief of Line by 60th Division will be completed by 6 a.m. July 14th aaa Addressed 51st Division repeated 60th Division.

XVII Corps.

Copies No 23 - 34 enclosed for distribution to your formations

Appendix C. 'G' Branch. HQ
WAR DIARY 60th DIVISION
JULY 1916.

*General Staff
Date 9-7-16
Reg. No. G/S.62.A
60th (LONDON) DIVISION*

S E C R E T.   Copy No. 19

51st (HIGHLAND) DIVISION.

OPERATION ORDER No.61.

Reference Map:-   8th July 1916.
    LENS 11. 1/100,000

1.   The 60th Division will relieve the 51st Division in the line during the period 11/17th July.

2.   The relief of the Infantry will be carried out in accordance with Table "A" attached. Relief to be completed by 6 a.m., 14th inst. XInstructions as regards handing and taking over of trench stores are republished for information.

        Brigadiers of 60th Division will take over Command of Brigade Sectors during the night 13/14th July on completion of the relief.

3.   The Artillery reliefs will be carried out on nights 14/15th, 15/16th and 16/17th July, under arrangements to be made between B.Gs. R.A., 51st Division and 60th Division.

        Six 18-pdr. and two 4'5" Howitzer Batteries 51st Divisional Artillery will remain in the line under the Command of G.O.C. 60th Division until further orders.

        On relief the 51st Divisional Artillery, less the above mentioned Batteries, will be withdrawn to the billetting areas shewn on the attached plan.

4.   The C.R.E., 51st Division will arrange that all special work now being carried on under him by the R.E. and Pioneers of the 60th Division is closed down by the night of the 11th inst.

5.   The Field Coys.R.E., 51st Division, will be relieved by Field Coys. R.E., 60th Division, as follows:-

    1/1st High.Fd.Co.R.E.   by   2/4th London Fd.Co.R.E.
    1/2nd High.Fd.Co.R.E.   by   3/3rd London Fd.Co.R.E.
    2/2nd High.Fd.Co.R.E.   by   1/6th London Fd.Co.R.E.

        Reliefs to take place on 12th and 13th July, under arrangements to be made by C.R.Es. of Divisions.

6.   The 1/12th Loyal North Lancs (Pioneers) will be withdrawn from the line on the 11th, and concentrated at MAROEUIL. On the 13th, 1 Company 1/12th Loyal North Lancs, will move into each Sector of the line, and take over from the 1/8th Royal Scots (Pioneers). On relief the 1/8th Royal Scots will withdraw to ECOIVRES.

X *will be issued later*

(2)

7.   The 152nd Infantry Brigade, 51st Division, will be billetted in ACQ and ECOIVRES, and will take over mining fatigues from the 60th Division before completion of relief. Headquarters at ECOIVRES.

This Brigade will be administered by the 60th Division.

The two Battalions not employed on mining fatigues will be in Corps Reserve.

8.   On relief the 51st Division (less 1 Infantry Brigade and 8 Batteries) will move to billets as shewn in March Table (Table "B") and billetting plan.

51st Division Headquarters will be at VILLERS CHATEL.

9.   Trench Mortar Batteries (Light and Medium) will be relieved during the nights 11/12th and 12/13th under arrangements to be made between the Brigadiers concerned.

The 51st Division will leave 1 Officer and 1 N.C.O. with each 2" Battery, and 2 Officers and 2 N.C.Os. with each Stokes Battery of the 60th Division for 24 hours after relief.

10.   Brigade Machine Guns will be relieved under arrangements to be made between Brigadiers concerned during nights 12/13th and 13/14th.

1 Officer in each Brigade of 51st Division and 1 man of each gun relieved, will remain for 24 hours with the 60th Division Machine Gun Companies.

11.   The O.C. 51st Divisional Signal Co. will arrange to leave with the Signal Co., 60th Division:-

    With Headquarters Section   -   1 Officer.
                                    3 Linesmen.

    With each Bde. Section   -   3 Linesmen.

These details will remain with the 60th Division for 3 days after completion of the relief.

12.   The 51st Divisional Grenade School and Physical Training School will close down on 12th inst., and will be handed over to 60th Division on 13th inst. The Gas School will close on the 13th inst., and be handed over on 14th inst.

13.   Mobile Vet. Section will move to TINQUES on 15th inst.

14.   Divisional Train (less 4th Company which remains in ACQ) will move to TINQUES under orders of D.A.Q.M.G.

/15

(3)

15.   Field Ambulances will be relieved under arrangements to be made by A.Ds.M.S. of 51st and 60th Divisions.
      Field Ambulances of 51st Division will move to new area under orders of D.A.Q.M.G.

16.   On arrival in Back Area Refilling Point for all units will be at TINQUES.

17.   The Command of the front will pass to G.O.C. 60th Division, at 10 a.m. 14th July.

D Baird Major
for Lieut.Colonel,
     General Staff,
     51st (Highland) Division.

Issued at 8 30 p.m.

Copy No. 1   152nd Infantry Bde.
         2   153rd Infantry Bde.
         3   154th Infantry Bde.
         4   C.R.A.
         5   C.R.E.
         6   "A".
         7   A.D.M.S.
         8   Signals.
         9   Divl. Train.
        10   8th Royal Scots.
        11   Divl. Supply Col.
        12   Divl. Amm. Col.
        13   A.D.C. for G.O.C.
        14   A.D.V.S.
        15   XVII Corps.
        16   "   "
        17   14th Division.
        18   2nd Division.
        19   30th Division.
        20   War Diary.
        21   File.
        22   Camp Commandant.

TABLE "A"

RELIEF OF 152nd INFANTRY BRIGADE BY 180th INFANTRY BRIGADE.

DATE.	5th SEA.HRS.	6th SEA.HRS.	6th GOR.HRS.	8th A.& S.H.	17th LON REGT.	18th LON REGT.	19th LON REGT.	20th LON REGT.	REMARKS.
10th July.	LEFT 1	LEFT 2	MT.ST.ELOY	OSTREVILLE	ACQ	REAR AREA.	BDE.RES. & TRENCHES.	BDE.RES. & TRENCHES.	PLATOON TRAINING.
11th July.	"	"	"	ECOIVRES.	"	MT.ST.ELOY & ACQ	"	"	COMPANY TRAINING.
12th July.	½MT.ST.ELOY & ½BDE.RES.	½MT.ST.ELOY & ½BDE.RES.	×NEUVILLE ST.VAAST.	×MAROEUIL & ANZIN.	"	MT.ST.ELOY.	½ BDE.RES. ½ Co.Training in LEFT 1.	LEFT 2.	
13th July.	ACQ.	×MONT.ST.ELOY & ACQ.	×	×	BDE.RES.	"	LEFT 1.	LEFT 2.	
14th July.	"	ECOIVRES.	×	×	"	MT.ST.ELOY. (Divl.Res).	"	"	

× Mining fatigues.

TABLE "A" RELIEF OF 153rd INFANTRY BRIGADE BY 179th INFANTRY BRIGADE.

DATE.	7th B.W.	6th B.W.	5th GOR.HRS.	7th GOR.HRS.	15th LON. REGT.	16th LON. REGT.	13th LON. REGT.	14th LON. REGT.	
11th July.	No.3 AREA	BRAY HUTS	CENTRE 2	CENTRE 1	NEUVILLE ST.VAAST.	MAROEUIL and ANZIN	½ BDE.RES. ½ TRENCHES	½ BDE.RES. ½ TRENCHES	
12th July.	"	No.3 AREA	ECOIVRES ½ BDE.RES.	½ CENTRE 1 ½ BDE.RES.	BRAY HUTS	BDE.RES.	X½ TRENCHES ½ BDE.RES.	CENTRE 2	X One day's extra Co. training
13th July.	"	"	No.3 AREA	ECOIVRES	BRAY HUTS (Div.Res)	"	CENTRE 1	"	
14th July.	"	"	"	No.3 AREA	"	"	"	"	

TABLE "A"   RELIEF OF 154th INFANTRY BRIGADE BY 181st INFANTRY BRIGADE.

DATE	4th SEA.HRS.	7th A.& S.H.	9th R.SCOTS.	4th GOR.HRS.	21st LON. REGT.	22nd LON. REGT.	23rd LON. REGT.	24th LON. REGT.
12th July.	RIGHT 1	RIGHT 2	ETRUN	MAROEUIL	BACK AREA	LOUEZ	½ BDE.RES. ½ BDE. TRENCHES	½ BDE.RES. ½ BDE. TRENCHES
13th July.	MAROEUIL	LOUEZ	No.2 AREA	No.2 AREA	ETRUN	BDE.RES.	RIGHT 1	RIGHT 2
14th July.	No.2 AREA	No.2 AREA	"	"	"	"	"	"

DATE.	UNIT.	FROM.	TO.	REMARKS.
13th July.	2/2nd Field Co. R.E.	MT.ST.ELOY	TINCQUETTE	
"	21st London Regt.	CHELERS	ETRUN	To march at 9 a.m. via TINQUES - ARRAS Road.
14th July.	7th Argylls	LOUEZ	No. 2 AREA	To march via ST. POL Road under orders
"	4th Seaforths	MAROEUIL	No. 2 AREA	of B.G.C. 154th Infantry Brigade.
"	154th Bde. T.M. Batts	ETRUN	No 2 AREA	Head of Column not to pass HAUTE AVESNES
"	154th Bde. M.G. Co.	ETRUN	No. 2 AREA	Cross Roads before 10.30 a.m.
"	7th Gordons	ECOIVRES	No. 3 AREA	To march at 9 a.m. via ACQ - AUBIGNY under orders of B.G.C. 153rd Infantry Brigade.
"	8th Royal Scots (less 2 Cos.)	ECOIVRES	TINQUES	To march at 10 a.m.
"	1 Co. 8th Royal Scots	ECOIVRES	BETHONSART	To march at 10 a.m.
"	1 Co. 8th Royal Scots	ECOIVRES	MINGOVAL	To march at 10 a.m.

TABLE "B"   MARCH TABLE ISSUED WITH OPERATION ORDER No. 61.

DATE.	UNIT.	FROM.	TO.	REMARKS.
11th July.	8th Argylls	OSTREVILLE	ECOIVRES	To march at 9 a.m.
"	18th London Regt.	VILLERS BRULIN	MT.ST.ELOY & ACQ	To arrive at 6 p.m.
12th July.	8th Argylls (less 2 Cos.)	ECOIVRES	MAROEUIL	To march at 9 a.m.
"	2 Cos. 8th Argylls	ECOIVRES	ANZIN	To march at 9 a.m.
"	6th Black Watch	BRAY HUTS	No. 3 AREA	To march at 9 a.m. via ACQ - AUBIGNY
13th July.	9th Royal Scots	ETRUN	No. 2 AREA	(To march via ST. POL Road under orders
"	4th Gordons	MAROEUIL	No. 2 AREA	(of B.G.C. 154th Infantry Brigade.
"	1/2nd Field Co. R.E.	ANZIN	No. 2 AREA	(Head of Column not to pass HAUTE AVESNES
"	5th Gordons	ECOIVRES	No. 3 AREA	(Cross Roads before 10.30 a.m.
"	153rd Bde. T.M. Batts.	ECOIVRES	No. 3 AREA	(
"	153rd Bde. M.G. Co.	BRAY	No. 3 Area	(To march at 9 a.m. via ACQ - AUBIGNY under
"	1/1st Field Co. R.E.	MAROEUIL	No. 3 AREA	(orders of B.G.C. 153rd Infantry Brigade.

P.T.O

SECRET

9th (Highland) Division
Billeting Map.
9th July 1916.

No. I. Area.
Div. H.Q.
Signal Co.   (Villers Chatel.
Pioneer Bn.   (Mingoral.
Conv. Co.   (Bethonsart.
2/1st Fd. Amb.   (Cambligneul.
San. Section.
Ad: Qm: R.E.

No. II Area.
H.Q.: 154th Inf. Bde.   (Chelers.
Machine Gun Co.   (Herlin-le-Vert.
T.M. Batteries.   (Le Tirlet.
4 Battalions.   (Guestreville.
1/2nd Fd. Co. R.E.   (Villers Brulin.
                        (Savy (Room for 1. Bn.)
                        (Bethencourt.

No. III Area.
H.Q.: 153rd Inf. Bde.   (Beilleul-Aux-Cornailles
Machine Gun Co.   (Monchy-Breton.
T.M. Batteries.   (Orlencourt.
4 Battalions.   (l'Abbaye de Neuville.
1/1st Fd. Co. R.E.   (Ostreville. Fme.
                        (Hostrel.
                        (Marquay.
                        (Boirin.

No. IV Area.
Div. Train (less 1 Co.) (Tinques.   (Capelle Fermont.
1/3rd Fd. Ambulance.   (Tincquette.   (Agnieres.
2/2nd Fd. Co. R.E.   (Roellecourt.
Mob. Vet. Section.

No. V Area.
Div. Art. (less 8 Batts)

60th Div. Area.
152nd Inf. Bde.
4th Co. Div. Train. (Ecoivres.
1/2nd Fd. Amb.   (Acq.
St. Michel-sur-Ternoire. 8 Batts. R.F.A.

Appendix D WAR DIARY
"G" Branch Hq 60th Division   JULY 1916.

SECRET.

51st (HIGHLAND) DIVISION.

AMENDMENT TO OPERATION ORDER No. 61.

1/8th Royal Scots move to MONCHY BRETON, and not as mentioned.

MONCHY BRETON will not be in 153rd Infantry Brigade Area.

Accommodation will be given for half Battalion 153rd Infantry Brigade at TINQUES.

Please acknowledge receipt.

Ian Stewart   Lieut.Colonel,
              General Staff,
              51st (HIGHLAND) DIVISION.

9th July 1916.

Copy sent to:-

    152nd Infantry Brigade.
    153rd Infantry Brigade.
    154th Infantry Brigade.
    C.R.A.
    C.R.E.
    "A".
    A.D.M.S.
    Signals.
    Divl. Train.
    8th Royal Scots.
    Divl. Supply Col.
    Divl. Amm. Col.
    A.D.C., for G.O.C.
    A.D.V.S.
    XVII Corps.
    14th Division.
    2nd Division.
    60th Division.
    War Diary.
    File.
    Camp Commandant.

TABLE "A".   RELIEF BY 179th INFANTRY BRIGADE OF 153rd INFANTRY BRIGADE.

DATE.	2/15 Lond. R.	2/16 Lond. R.	2/14 Lond. R.	2/15 Lond. R.	7th B.W.	6th B.W.	5th GOR. HRS.	7th GOR. HRS.
11th July.	NEUVILLE ST. VAAST.	MAROEUIL & ANZIN.	½ BDE. RES. ½ TRENCHES.	½ BDE. RES. ½ TRENCHES.	No. 3 AREA.	BRAY HUTS.	CENTRE 2.	CENTRE 1.
12th July.	BRAY HUTS.	BDE. RES.	"	CENTRE 2.	"	No. 3 AREA.	ECOIVRES.	½ CENTRE 1 ½ BDE. RES.
13th July.	BRAY HUTS. (DIV. RES.)	"	CENTRE 1.	"	"	"	No. 3 AREA.	ECOIVRES.
14th July.	"	"	"	"	"	"	"	No. 3 AREA.

TABLE "A"   RELIEF BY 180th INFANTRY BRIGADE OF 152nd INFANTRY BRIGADE.

DATE.	2/17 Lond. R.	2/18 Lond. R.	2/19 Lond. R.	2/20 Lond. R.	5th SEA.HRS.	6th SEA.HRS.	6th GOR.HRS.	8th A.& S.H.	REMARKS.
10th July.	ACQ.	REAR AREA.	BDE.RES. & TRENCHES.	BDE.RES. & TRENCHES.	LEFT 1.	LEFT 2.	Mt.St. ELOY.	OSTREVILLE.	
11th July.	"	Mt.St. ELOY & ACQ.	"	"	"	"	"	ECOIVRES.	
12th July.	"	Mt.St. ELOY.	½ BDE. RES. ½ Co. Training in LEFT 1	LEFT 2.	"	½ Mt.St. ELOY. ½ Bde. RES.	NEUVILLE ST.VAAST.*	MAROEUIL & ANZIN.	
13th July.	BDE.RES.	"	LEFT 1.	"	ACQ.	Mt.St. ELOY & ACQ.	" *	" *	
14th July.	"	Mt.St. ELOY. (Div.Res)	"	"	"	ECOIVRES.	" *	" *	

* Mining Fatigues.

TABLE "A"   RELIEF BY 181st INFANTRY BRIGADE OF 154th INFANTRY BRIGADE.

DATE.	2/21 Lond. R.	2/22 Lond. R.	2/23 Lond. R.	2/24 Lond. R.	4th SEA. HRS.	7th A & S.H.	9th R.SCOTS.	4th GOR.HRS.
12th July.	BACK AREA.	LOUEZ.	BDE.RES. BDE. TRENCHES. 1/2+1/2	BDE.RES. BDE. TRENCHES. 1/2+1/2	RIGHT 1.	RIGHT 2.	ETRUN.	MAROEUIL.
13th July.	ETRUN.	BDE.RES.	RIGHT 1.	RIGHT 2.	MAROEUIL.	LOUEZ.	No. 2 AREA.	No. 2 AREA.
14th July.	"	"	"	"	No. 2 AREA.	No. 2 AREA.	"	"

TRENCH STORES. Appendix "B".

The following are permanent trench stores and will be taken over by incoming Units. All stores which are being repaired by Ordnance are being accounted for by Bdes. to be relieved.

Bombs (those stored in trenches only)
Bomb throwers.
Boots gum thigh.
Braziers.
Barrels, water.
Buckets, earth (or pails earth)
Buckets, Latrine.
Brooms.
Catapults.
Costumes, Camouflage.
" Snipers.
" Acid proof.
Grenades. (those in trenches only).
Gongs and apparatus for warning Gas attacks.
Loophold plates.
Ladders.
Lights, Very (those stored in trenches only)
Megaphones.
Receptacles for water.
Rods, measuring.
Rammers.
Rifle Rests.
Rockets and stands.
Rifle Batteries (the rifles are Regt. equip)
Stands, rifle grenade.
S.A.A.Reserves (any reserves kept in the trenches and not on the man)
Salvus breathing sets.
Syringes.

Soyers Stoves.
Stretchers, Trench.
Scoops, water.
Sticks, microphone.
Tapes, measuring.
Tapes, tracing.
Telephone wire (in situ.)
Trench Mortars not in batteries.
Weather cocks.
Washing basins.
Wire barbed and plain.
Wheelbarrows and hand barrows.
Vermorel Sprayers.
Veils Observers.
Hot food containers.
Bomb Boxes.
Hand Sprayers.
Pails.
Thermos boxes.
Hose lengths.
Hyperscopes.

P.T.O.

2.

R.E. Stores (Entrenching tools, and all items obtained
(from R.E. Parks (except those held on charge
(of units under Mobn. Store tables) such as Axes,
(felling, Bill Hooks, Crowbars, Chisels, Hammers,
(Mauls, Picks, Pumps, and mining tools, Reaping
(Hooks and sickles, saws, shovels, and spades,
(boring tools, Hoes, Mud Scrapers

The following Brigade and Regimental Stores are being taken out by Brigades and Battalions on relief :-

Very Pistols.
Illuminating Pistols.
Periscopes (Regtz Equip.)
Telephone Equipment (except wires in situ.)
Rifles and Telescopic Sights.
Phosphorescent Night Sights.
Machine Gun Stove Pipe Attachments.
Grenade Carriers.
Signalling Discs.
Portable Machine Gun Mountings.
Elephant Rifles.
Pliers wire   ) up to numbers allowed
Hedging Gloves) as Regt. Equipment.
Wire Cutters.
Hills Optical Sights.
G.O.C's Telescopic Rifles.
Grenade Rifles.
Box Respirators.

10th July 1916.

Lieut-Colonel,
General Staff,
60th (London) Division.

SECRET.

Amendment, Defence Scheme.

Page 1, 3rd line from bottom :-
    Centre Art. Group H.Q. ... Moisoneuse (F.30.a.6.8)
Page 2, 12th line, for Maroeuil read Louez.
Acknowledge.

60th Div.H.Q.,
11th July 1916.

                         Captain,
                        General Staff.

Appendix F

CERTIFIED TRUE COPY.

SECRET.

51st Division.
60th Division.
B.G.R.A.
"Q"
                                                G.248   14/7/16.

    Reference XVII Corps order No. 16 of 17th July the reliefof the Artillery 51st Division by that of 60th Division will be completed tonight aaa Stripped guns will be exchanged aaa Batteries of 51st Divisional Artillery will proceed to their wagon lines aaa Addressed 51st and 60th Divisions and B.G.R.A.

XVII Corps.   (Sgd) J. MACKENZIE. Major,
1.30 p.m.   General Staff.

Appendix "E"
WAR DIARY HQ 60th Division
JULY 1916 'G' Branch War diary

SECRET.

Copy No. 19.

60th DIVISION ORDER No. 1.

10th July 1916.

(1) The 60th Div. will relieve the 51st Div. in the line during the period 11th to 17th July.

(2) The relief of the Infantry will be carried out in accordance with the attached tables. Reliefs are to be completed by 6 a.m., 14th inst. Bde. Commanders will take over Command of Sectors on completion of relief during the night of 13th/14th July.
   Guides from Units to be relieved will be provided and the time and place where they will meet relieving troops will be arranged between Bde. Commanders.

(3) The Artillery reliefs will be carried out on nights 14th/15th, 15th/16th and 16th/17th under arrangements between the two B.G's., R.A. concerned.
   * 16th/17th
   Six 18 pdr., and two 4.5" Howitzer Battys., 51st Div. are remaining in the line.
   The D.A.C. will move to Capelle Forment on the 17th under the orders of the C.R.A.

(4) T.H. Battys. (Light & Medium) will relieve those of the 51st Div. during the nights 11th/12th and 12th/13th under arrangements to be made between Bde. Commanders concerned.

(5) The Fd. Cos. R.E. will relieve the Fd. Cos. R.E., 51st Div. on the 12th and 13th July under arrangements between C.R.E's concerned.

(6) Bde. M.G. Cos. will relieve those of the 51st Div. during the nights 12th/13th and 13th/14th under arrangements to be made between Bde. Commanders concerned.

(7) The 1/12th L.N.Lancs. R. will concentrate at Maroeuil and Louez on the 11th. On the 13th one Co. will relieve one Co. 1/8th Royal Scots in each Sector. The H.Q. and remaining Co. of the Bn. will be in Louez.

(8) The Field Ambs. will relieve those of the 51st Div. under arrangements between the A.D's.M.S. concerned. They will be located as under:-

   2/4th Fd. Amb.........Ecoivres.
   2/5th & 2/6th Fd. Ambs..Haute d'Avesnes.

   The San. Sec. will move to Hermaville on the 14th under the orders of the A.D.M.S.

(9) The Mob. Vet. Sec. will relieve the Mob. Vet. Sec. of the 51st Div. on the Arras - St. Pol road, half mile S. of Aubigny on the 15th inst. under the orders of the A.D.V.S.

(10) The Train will move as follows, under the orders of the A.Q.M.G.:-

   Det. No. 1 Co., Nos. 2 and 4 Cos. to Haute d'Avesnes.
   No. 3 Co.   to Acq.

-2-

(11)　　A List of Trench Stores handed over will be given to incoming Units. A List showing permanent, Brigade and Regimental Stores is attached. (App. "B").

(12)　　The 51st Div. is leaving behind the following personnel. Arrangements are to be made for their rations and quartering:-

For 24 Hours.

    1 Off. and 1 N.C.O. with each Medium T.M.Batty.
    2 Off. and 2 N.C.O's with each Light T.M.Batty.
    1 Off. (per Bde.) with each Bde. M.G.Co.
    1 man (per gun relieved) with each Bde. M.G.Co.

For 3 days.

    1 Off. and 3 Linesmen with   H.Q. Sec. Signal Co.
            3　"　　with each Bde. Sec. Signal Co.
    1 Off. and 8 N.C.O's with each Bn.

(13)　　The 152nd Inf. Bde. and No. 4/Co., 51 Div. Train, will be billetted in Acq and Ecoivres and will be administered by this Div.   H.Q. at Ecoivres.
    2 Bns. of this Bde. will relieve the 2/15 and 2/16 London Regiments respectively on the night of the 12th/13th July.

(14)　　Orders as regards the administration of Units in the Div. Area, other than those belonging to the 51st or 60th Divs. will be issued later.

(15)　　On arrival in the line, refilling points will be as under:-

    Acq. -　180th Inf. Bde. (including Bde. M.G.Co, 180 Light and Y Medium T.M.Battys.), 1/6th Fd. Co. R.E., 2/4th Fd. Amb. and No. 3 Co., Div. Train.
    Haute d'Avesnes.-　All other Units of the Div.

(16)　　The Command of the Front remains in the hands of the G.O.C., 51st Div. until 10 a.m., 14th July.

(17)　　60th Div. H.Q. will be established at Hermaville at 10 a.m., 14th July.

(18)　　Acknowledge.

H.Q., 60th Div.　　　　　　　　　　　　　　　Lieut-Colonel.
10th July 1916.　　　　　　　　　　　　　　　General Staff.

Copies issued at........
    to:-
    No. 1.　179 Inf. Bde.　　　No. 12. A.D.C.
        2.　180　"　　"　　　　　　13. A.D.V.S.
        3.　181　"　　"　　　　　　14 &
        4.　C.R.A.　　　　　　　　　15. 17 Corps.
        5.　C.R.E.　　　　　　　　　16. 14th Div.
        6.　"A".　　　　　　　　　　17. 2nd Div.
        7.　A.D.M.S.　　　　　　　　18. 51st Div.
        8.　Signals.　　　　　　　　19. War Diary.
        9.　1/12 L.N.Lancs. R.　　　20. File.
      10.　Div. Train.　　　　　　　21. Camp Commandant.
      11.　Div. Supply Col.

Appendix G
WAR DIARY JULY 1916
G. Branch HQ 60th Division.   Copy No. 17.

SECRET.

DEFENCE SCHEME (PROVISIONAL).

1. The line to be held by this Division extends from the point where the avenue Ab del Kader cuts the front line N. of Roclincourt (inc.) to the Avenue Central (exc.). (Trenches L.20 – P.79, both inc.)

    The 14th Division is on the right and the 2nd Division on the left of the Divisional Line.

2. The line is organised for defence as follows:-

    (a). Front Line system which is subdivided into:-

       (i). Observation Line, which consists of advanced posts on Craters or in sap heads.
       (ii). Firing Line: A continuous line immediately in rear of the observation line. This is the main line of resistance and is to be held to the last.
       (iii). Support line: A line immediately in rear of the firing line at a distance varying from 80 to 100 yards, provided with strong points.
       (iv). Reserve line; Including the fortified post of Ecurie, Work A, Work B, Fork Redoubt, Elbe Trench and Nouville St. Vaast. This line is supported by the work at Maison Blanche.

    (b). Corps Line running from St. Aubin Northwards and passing just E. of Berthonval Wood.

    (c). Army Line running N. and S. just E. of Haute-Avesnes.

3. Delimitation of Sectors.

    The line is divided into three sectors as per attached map. Sector Commanders are responsible for the defence and up-keep of areas as shown. They have no responsibility as regards Corps and Army Lines.

    The Front Lines and Main Communication Trenches are as follows:-

    Right Sector.
        From the Avenue Ab del Kader (Trench L.20) to Trench M.33 (both inc.)
        C.T's: Genie, Anzin and Aniversaire Avenues.

    Centre Sector.
        From Trench M.34 to where Trench O.61 cuts Lichfield Avenue (both inc.)
        C.T's: Vase Sapeur, and Territorial Avenues.

    Left Sector.
        From where Trench O.61 cuts Lichfield Avenue (exc.) to Trench P.79 (inc.)
        C.T's: Denis le Rock, and Pont St.

4. Distribution of Troops.
    (i) Right Sector.
        181 Inf. Bde.   H.Q.   Etrun.
                                     Adv. H.Q.   G.9.b.2.9.
                                     Reserve Bn.   Etrun.
                                     H.Q.   G.9.b.2.9.
        Right Art. Group.   H.Q.   Anzin.
        3/3 Fd. Co. R.E.   Anzin &
        1 Co. Pioneer Bn.   Louez.

    (ii). Centre Sector.
        179 Inf. Bde.   H.Q.   Ecoivres.
                                     Adv. H.Q.   A.8.d.2.5.
                                     Reserve Bn.   Maroeuil. Bray
                                     H.Q.   Madagascar.
        Centre Art. Group.   H.Q.   Maroeuil.
        2/4 Fd. Co. R.E.   Ariane.
        1 Co. Pioneer Bn.

-2-

(iii). **Left Sector.**

180 Inf. Bde.	H.Q.	Mont St. Eloy.
	Adv. H.Q.	A.8.c.7.9.
	Reserve Bn.	~~Bray~~ Mt. St. Eloy.
Left Art. Group.	H.Q.	Berthonval.
1/6 Fd. Co. R.E.	H.Q.	Mont St. Eloy.
1 Co. Pioneer Bn.		Neuville St. Vaast.

The Reserve Bn. in each Sector will form the Divisional Reserve.

(iv). The Pioneer Bn. has 3 Cos. allotted to Sectors as above. The H.Q. and remaining Co. of the Bn. is located at Maroeuil.

5. Communications.

   (a). The following telephonic communications exist:-

   Cos. in Front Line with Bn. H.Q.
   Bn. H.Q. with Bde. H.Q. and Bns. on their flanks.
   Bde. H.Q. with Div. H.Q. and with the Artillery Group allotted to their Sector. (Note: The Code Words of those Groups are Right, Centre and Left Group, respectively.
   Art. Groups with C.R.A. to whom they should apply for the co-operation of the Heavy Artillery.

   Bns. in the Front Line are connected to Batteries through Artillery Liaison Officers, and, in some cases, companies in the Front Line are connected by telephone to the Battery which covers them.

6. Action in case of Attack.

   In the event of a serious attack, the following arrangements will be carried out:-

   (a). Staffs.

   Adv. H.Q. will be established as follows:-
   Div. H.Q....Etrun, with command post at A.26.b.7.4.
   Sector Commanders to the places named in para. 4.

   (b). Sectors.

   In case of a heavy bombardment, the firing line will not be reinforced. All troops in the lines which are being shelled should take cover in dug-outs, etc., with the exception of sentries and 2 men per Lewis or Machine Gun, until the alarm is given that the enemy are advancing.

   The garrison at Ecurie will be reinforced by one Co. of the Div. Reserve under the orders of the G.O.C., 181 Inf. Bde.

   Sector Commanders must make arrangements for meeting all forms of attack, and will ensure that Commanders of all strong points know their duties and that the garrisons of the same man their defences once during their tour of occupation.

   Should the enemy succeed in penetrating any part of our line, a counter-attack is to be organised at once to eject him. This counter-attack should, as a rule, be organised by the Commander on the spot, so that it may be carried out rapidly and thus deny to the enemy the necessary time to consolidate the position he has won. Counter-attacking troops should invariably have strong parties of bombers.

The minimum garrisons of fortified posts in the Reserve Line, viz., Ecurie, Maison Blanche and Nouville St. Vaast are on no account to be employed in counter-attacks.

The Bns. in Div. Reserve will assemble on their alarm posts but will not be moved (except the Co. of the 181 Inf Bde. mentioned above) without authority from Div. H.Q.

(c). Pioneers.

The O.C., Pioneer Bn. will send up the Co. of Pioneers from Maroeuil and 4 Lewis Guns to reinforce the garrison at Maison Blanche.

The O.C., Pioneer Bn. will then assume command of this garrison.

The remaining 4 Lewis Guns will be sent to Nouville St. Vaast.

Cos. allotted to the various sectors will act under the orders of the Sector Commanders. Their general rôle should be as reserves to the garrisons of the strong points in the sectors in which they are working.

(d). R.E.

The Field and Tunnelling Cos. will Stand to Arms in their billets. Detachments working in the trenches will act under the orders of the Commander of the Sector in which they are working.

(e). Warning.

A priority message "ATTACK QUARTERS" will be sent when necessary to bring this scheme into operation.

(f). Gas Alarm.

On hearing the Gas Alarm or on receiving the G.A.S. message, the procedure will be the same as for "ATTACK QUARTERS", except that troops will keep out of dug-outs and shelters.

7. Defence of Second Line.

In the event of a withdrawal to the Corps Line being ordered, Brigadiers will be responsible for holding the portions of that line already enumerated as in their sectors. - (para. 3c.)

8. Mining Fatigues.

Right Sector.

The party having its H.Q. at Abri Centrale A.28.b.3.8. will remain there as Bde. Reserve, men actually at work in the shafts, rejoining at this place via Down Trench.

Centre Sector.

The Co. will be disposed as follows:-
1 Platoon as garrison to "B" redoubt.
1   "   "   "   " Fork   "
2 Platoons await orders at Sapper Shelter.

-4-

Left Sector.

The whole of this Bn. in Neuville St. Vaast will form the garrison of that place. Men actually working in shafts withdrawing thither as soon as possible.

9. The following appendices are attached:-

(a) Destination of troops in Div. Reserve (if ordered). Routes to the same and times required to reach destination.

(b) Battle Straggler Posts and Custody of Prisoners.

(c) Garrisons of defended localities.

H.Q., 60th Div.
July 1916.

Lieut-Colonel.
General Staff.

APPENDIX "A".

MOVEMENTS OF TROOPS IN DIVISIONAL RESERVE TO POSITIONS OF ASSEMBLY.

UNIT.	FROM.	TO.	ROUTE.	TIME REQUIRED TO REACH DESTINATION.	REMARKS.
(1). 1 Co. 181 Inf. Bde	Etrun.	Ecurie.	Anzin Avenue.	$1\frac{1}{4}$ hours.	
(2). 1 Bn. 181 Inf. Bde. (less 1 Co.)	Etrun.	Corps Line Trenches N. of St. Aubin.	Anzin Road.	1 hour.	
(3). Pioneer Bn. 1 Co.	Maroeuil.	Maison Blanche.	Profond Val Avenue - Moissoneuse - Sapper Avenue.	$2\frac{1}{4}$ hours.	
(4). 1 Bn. 180 Inf. Bde	Maroeuil.	Group of old works just W. of Maison Blanche. (Moissoneuse)	As above, halting at Moissoneuse.	$2\frac{1}{2}$ hours.	
(5). 1 Bn. 179 Inf. Bde	Bray.	Fort George.	Pont Street.	$1\frac{1}{2}$ hours.	

APPENDIX "B"

BATTLE STRAGGLER POSTS - CUSTODY OF PRISONERS.

In the case of active operations:-

1. Battle Straggler Posts will be organised in the Division as follows:-

(a). BRIGADE POSTS.

Posts will be established under Brigade arrangements along the Bethune - Arras Road.

Should the Divisional Front be broken, these Posts will re-assemble on the line of the Divisional Posts as follows:-

Louez - Maroeuil - Bray - Mont St. Eloy.

(b). DIVISIONAL POSTS.

Posts will be placed at the following points:-

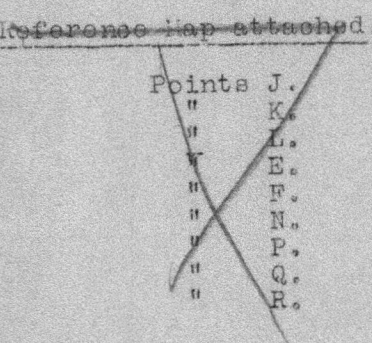

Reference Map 51c. 1/40,000.	~~Reference Map attached.~~
L.8.b.3.9.	Points J.
L.9.b.2.7.	" K.
L.4.a.5.6.	" L.
F.28.c.3.5.	" E.
F.28.a.2.9.	" F.
F.15.d.8.1.	" N.
F.9.c.10.0.	" P.
F.9.a.5.4.	" Q.
F.9.a.0.10.	" R.

COLLECTING STATIONS.

To which unwounded stragglers will be conducted will be formed at the Headquarters of the Bns. in Div. Reserve, and will be under the Quartermasters of those Bns. They will be sent back to their Units from here under an officer or N.C.O.

2. PRISONERS.

Prisoners will be taken over from Inf. Bdes. under Corps arrangements at Anzin Church, Maroeuil Church and Bray Huts.

APPENDIX "C".

DEFENDED LOCALITIES.

Name of Work.	Garrison. Permanent.	Maximum.	Machine Guns.	Lewis Rifle.	Reserve. S.A.A.	Grenades.	Rations.	Remarks.
Ecurie	2 Cos.	3 Cos.	2.	6.	252000	1500	2 days.	
A. Redoubt.	1 Platoon.	2 Platoons	"	1	10000.	120.	"	Under construction.
B. Redoubt.	1 Platoon.	2 Platoons	"	1	10000.	120.	"	Under construction.
Bentata.	1 Platoon.	2 Platoons	1.		20000.	240.	"	
Zivy.	1 Platoon.	2 Platoons	1.		20000.	240.	"	
Maison Blanche.	1 Company.	2 Cos.	4	6.	252000.	750.	"	
Neuville St. Vaast.	1 Bn.	2 Bns.	6	8	294000.	3000.	"	
Palace.	1 Platoon.	2 Platoons	1	"	18000.	90.	"	Under construction.
Empire.	1 Platoon	2 Platoons	1	"	18000.	180.	"	Under construction.

APPENDIX "D".

ARRANGEMENTS FOR EVACUATING CASUALTIES FROM FRONT AREA.

(1). 2/4 Lond. Amb. collects and evacuates casualties from the Left and Centre Sectors. 2/6 Lond. Amb. from the Right Sector.

(2). Left and Centre Sectors.
    (a). Collecting Posts are at :-
        (i). A.8.b.6.8. Neuville St. Vaast.
        (ii). A.9.c.1.5. Post Centrale.
    (b). Advanced Dressing Station for this Area is at A.8.c.5.5. Aux Rietz.

    (c). Evacuation from Aux Rietz to Main Dressing Station is by ambulance car at night; by Territorial Avenue by day. In case of extreme urgency and if conditions permit, car may go to Aux Rietz by day.

(3). Right Sector.
    (a). Collecting Posts are at:-
        (i). A.28.c.1.1. Route de Lille.
        (ii). A.26.d.9.4. Madagascar.
        (iii). A.20.d.5.7. near Ariane.
    (b). Advanced Dressing Station for this Area is at G.7.b.8.8. Anzin St. Aubin.

(4). The Divisional Rest Station formed by 2/5 Lond. Amb. is at Haute Avesnes.

(5). Medical Officers in charge of Units, on taking over an Aid Post, should immediately report their arrival and exact position of Aid Post, by Map reference if possible, to the Officer in Charge, Advanced Dressing Station.

(6). Units which are not actually in the Trenches, yet stationed in the Front Area (such as Batteries) will likewise communicate with Advanced Dressing Stations to secure the removal of casualties.

(7). These arrangements apply to the collection of Sick as well as wounded.

(8). A Medical Inspection Room as been established in Maroeuil for the details billetted in Maroeuil who have no Medical Officers. A Medical Officer will be there daily from 9 a.m. to 10 a.m.

H.Q., 60th Div.
11th July 1916.

Lieut-Colonel.
General Staff.

S E C R E T.   Appendix B   Copy No. 6

WAR DIARY JULY 1916
"G" Branch, HQ 60th DIVISION
XVII CORPS ORDER No. 16.

7th July, 1916.

Reference 1/100,000 LENS Sheet.

1. The 60th Division will relieve the 51st Division under inter-divisional arrangements.

2. (a) The relief of the 51st Division (less artillery) will be completed by 6 a.m. on the 14th July.

(b) The artillery reliefs will be carried out on nights 14th/15th, 15th/16th and 16th/17th July.

Six 18-pdr. and two 4.5" howitzer batteries, 51st Divisional Artillery, will remain in the line under the command of G.O.C. 60th Division until further orders.

(c) The command of the front will pass to 60th Division at 10 a.m. July 14th.

3. (a) On relief 51st Division (less 1 infantry brigade and eight batteries) will move to the area shown on the attached map.

51st Division Headquarters will be at VILLERS-CHATEL.

(b) One infantry brigade 51st Division will be billetted in ACQ and ECOIVRES and will take over the mining fatigues from 60th Division before completion of infantry relief. Headquarters at ECOIVRES. This brigade will be administered by 60th Division. The two battalions not employed in mining fatigues will be in Corps reserve.

4. Separate instructions will be issued regarding the dates on which working parties of the 60th Division now employed under the Chief Engineer and the 51st Division will rejoin their own division.

5. Progress of relief to be reported to XVII Corps Headquarters.

Brigadier-General.
General Staff.

Issued to Signals at 7.15 a.m.

Copy No.   to Third Army.
              IV Corps.
              VI Corps.
              Controller of Mines, Third Army.
              51st Division.
              60th Division.
              C.E.
              B.G.R.A.
              Corps Heavy Artillery.
              D.A.& Q.M.G.
              D.D.M.S.
              Signals.
              War Diary.
              File.

SECRET.

Vol 3

War Diary
of
General Staff Branch.
60th (London) Division.
From 1st August 1916
To 31st August 1916.
Volume III.

SECRET   Gen: Staff   60th Division   August 1916.

Army Form C. 2118

WAR DIARY
or
INTELLIGENCE SUMMARY
(Erase heading not required.)

Instructions regarding War Diaries and Intelligence Summaries are contained in F. S. Regs., Part II. and the Staff Manual respectively. Title Pages will be prepared in manuscript.

Place	Date	Hour	Summary of Events and Information	Remarks and references to Appendices
HERMAVILLE	1st	4.40am	Division report situation normal. Enemy T.M. active on GRANGE crater & silenced by artillery	CMB / EM
"	"	4.50pm	Division report situation quiet, nothing to report	CMB
"	"		Weather fine. Wind N.E.	
"	2nd	4.45am	Division report situation normal.	CMB
"	"	2.6pm	Division report British aeroplane was hit and landed at G.9.b.2.9. at 1.15pm. Pilot safe. Hostile artillery opened fire on the aeroplane and it is now in flames	CMB
"	"	4.5pm	Division report situation unchanged. Our artillery and trench mortars bombarded SPOONER crater at 10.45am with satisfactory results.	CMB
"	"		Weather fine. Wind hot from E. to N.E. and changes to W. about midday.	CMB
"	"	7am	Two hostile aeroplanes appeared over the neighbourhood — one driven off by our machines	"
"	3rd	4.55am	Division report situation normal. Considerable hostile T.M. activity on Right sector between 8.30pm and 11pm. Otherwise quiet.	CMB
"	"	5.1pm	Division report situation unchanged. Hostile artillery somewhat active against right of Centre sector about noon. Otherwise quiet.	CMB
"	"	10/pm	Enemy shelled horse lines & billets at ACQ for about one hour with 15 c.m. gun without any loss.	CMB
"	"		Corps Heavy Artillery retaliated by shelling VILLERVAL	CMB
"	"		Weather fine & hot. Wind N.W.	CMB
"	4th	4.35am	Situation quiet. Division report situation quiet. ACQ was shelled last night between 10 and 11 p.m.	CMB
"	"	5pm	Division report situation quiet. Continued artillery and T.M. shoot carried out on B14 crater and hostile trenches in vicinity at 11am with apparently successful results. Enemy shelled crossroads A8c66. both at 2h before between 1.45 and 3.30pm. No damage done.	CMB
"	"		Weather fine. Wind N.+N.W.	CMB
"	5th	4.35am	Division report situation unchanged.	CMB
"	"	3.26pm	All Infantry Brigades warned that Gas Alert is ordered forthwith from Div: on our right and orders to have all Concerned at once.	CMB
"	"	5pm	Division report situation quiet. Eight enemy balloons up opposite our front one very close N.E. of THELUS. Weather fine in the afternoon raining cloudy morning wind N.E.	CMB

1875 Wt. W593/826 1,000,000 4/15 J.B.C. & A. A.D.S.S./Forms/C. 2118.

Army Form C. 2118

WAR DIARY
or
INTELLIGENCE SUMMARY
(Erase heading not required.)

Instructions regarding War Diaries and Intelligence Summaries are contained in F. S. Regs., Part II. and the Staff Manual respectively. Title Pages will be prepared in manuscript.

Place	Date	Hour	Summary of Events and Information	Remarks and references to Appendices
HERMAVILLE	6th	12.15am	Right Group Artillery and 181st Inf Bde reported heavy bombardment on our front right front. In rear of Telephone conversations between Division and 21st Div on right, Divisional Artillery agreed to 2 S/Ds	apx
"	"	12.35am	"21st Div"	apx
"	"	12.58am	Division inform 17th Corps of bombardment and report that 21st Div now say all is quiet.	apx
"	"	4.58am	Division report situation unchanged. Enemy flares/cannonfire at Saunters morning. N. of CESSARY crater.	apx
"	"	4.58pm	Division report situation unchanged. Enemy batteries at F.5.d.4.5. heavily shelled during morning but no damage or casualties. One of our batteries returned to German front line trenches between A.10.b.4.10 and A.4.a.4.2	apx
"	"	10.30pm	2/13 Bn Gordon Regt carried out raid on German front line trenches and had settling barrage.	apx
"	"	12 mn	News received that all the party making the raid Gordon trenches and had spent a barrage with TM's but then right from artillery had been fired. The enemy did not a barrage. One prisoner taken. One trench Walker crater & June. Wound N.E.	apx
"	7th	5.55am	Division report situation unchanged. Quite active report enemy's line raided at 10.30pm and one prisoner taken. Right sector report for Sidney trench TM's active in their left front.	apx
"	"	9am	Division report further details of raid. Party entered left our trenches practically according to programme, but unfortunately those party fell into deep hole and kept returning. Enfiladed German Rifle fire. One party one German killed and brought in. After capturing in trench knocked about one prisoner captured - 6 to 8c, rifles, etc. Left German trench, trench party ordered to withdraw owing to accident. Our casualties 2 off + 12 mn killed 2 off + 12 mm 27 o/ranks, of which 5 were wounded	A 23 d 10.67
"	"	5pm	Division report situation unchanged. Quiet day	apx
"	"	9.30pm	2/10 Bn J. Reg. carried out raid on German front line trench between A.23 c 99.17 and A.23 d 10.67	apx
"	"		Weather cool & fine. Wind N.E.	apx
"	8th	5.17am	Division report situation now quiet. On the right sector, we raided the enemy's trench at 9.30pm. Three were mines laid with bag work fired. Trench but considerably damaged by our fire. Enemy's barrage fell for some time. One of our party was slightly delayed by drill fire and enemy Rifle fire. Our party R2 Bn & 4 Batten Bn had front and south four dugouts. Only one German seen.	apx

1875 Wt. W593/826 1,000,000 4/15 J.B.C. & A. A.D.S.S./Forms/C. 2118.

Army Form C. 2118

WAR DIARY
or
INTELLIGENCE SUMMARY

(Erase heading not required.)

Instructions regarding War Diaries and Intelligence Summaries are contained in F.S. Regs., Part II. and the Staff Manual respectively. Title Pages will be prepared in manuscript.

Place	Date	Hour	Summary of Events and Information	Remarks and references to Appendices
HERMAVILLE	8th	7.33am	Division report to 17th Corps that one officer & O.R. previously missing on night 6th/7th have come in and 2 O.R. reported killed.	Cps
"	"	4.57/pm	Division report quiet day and no unusual activity anywhere. Weather fine. Wind E. nobbly.	Cpd
"	"	4.35am	Division report situation unchanged. Except for poor rifle grenades in left sector the night was very quiet.	Cpd
"	9th	4.55pm	Division enemy shelled A8c.1.5 with 4·2" between 11am and 3pm and communication trenches near S.27. S.22. between 11 and 11.30am. Some damage to trenches. Otherwise quiet on rest of front.	Cpd
"	"	7.22pm	Division report to 17 Corps enemy flew camouflet opposite left 1 at 4.57pm. Position not yet located. Weather fine, wind light variable.	Cpd
"	10th	4.35am	Division report MONT ST ELOY observation post at 3.15pm. The Makers. MtKING revisited MONT ST ELOY observation post at 3.15pm.	Cpd
"	"	9.30am	Division report situation unchanged	Cpd
"	"	9.46am	Division report no trace to be found above ground of camouflet but mining galleries blown in.	Cpd
"	"		17th Corps ask for exact position of camouflet.	Cpd
"	"	4.3pm	Division report camouflet blown against Q sub P75. (S28a 43 48) COMMONS crater.	Cpd
"	"	4.53pm	Division report quiet day. Weather dull, hazy rest in early morning, changing to fine. Wind N.W.	Cpd
"	11th	12.30am	Mine blown by us about A4b 25 30.	Cpd
"	"	1am	179 Inf Bde report craters 54/13ed and consolidation in progress.	Cpd
"	"	5.50am	Division report we exploded mine at A4d 25.30. at 12.30am. Both lips were at once occupied the rear lip being in progress of consolidation. Enemy quiet except for bursts of M.G. fire he carried out bombardment of enemy front line at A10d 1.5 to distract attention from mine between 12.30 and 12.35am. Quiet otherwise.	Cpd
"	"	5.5pm	Division report situation normal. Weather hazy in early morning turning to very hot & fine about 9am. Wind N.W.	Cpd
"	12th	4.40am	Division report situation unchanged.	Cpd
"	"	4.44pm	Division report situation quiet. Weather fine, hazy in early morning	Cpd

WAR DIARY
or
INTELLIGENCE SUMMARY

Army Form C. 2118

(Erase heading not required.)

Instructions regarding War Diaries and Intelligence Summaries are contained in F.S. Regs., Part II. and the Staff Manual respectively. Title Pages will be prepared in manuscript.

Place	Date	Hour	Summary of Events and Information	Remarks and references to Appendices
HERMAVILLE	13th	5.17a.m.	Division report 16/17 Corps. We raided enemy trenches at S.28.c.6.9. at 2am. App. have found cart and trenches badly damaged. Dugouts were empty, only 2 Germans were seen and no identifications were secured. Whole party returned with 3 slightly wounded. No hostile M.G. & little rifle fire. Centre sector was bombarded by T.M's between 2.30 and 3am. All telephone wires on left subsector cut. In right sector enemy heavily bombarded the left subsector with T.M's + H.E shells. 8 patrols have been out.	Appx
"	"	4.37pm	Division report situation quiet. Weather fine. Wind N.East.	Appx
"	14th	4.25am	Division report situation normal.	Appx
"	"	2.35pm	Division report. Enemy sprung mine about S.28.a.4.8. at 8am this morning. Small mound formed. Completely commanded by TIDZA. No tactical importance.	Appx
"	"	4.45pm	Division report hostile 8" Howitzer Battery shelled two of our batteries in G.10.c at 10.15am and 2.15pm doing some damage. Situation otherwise quiet.	Appx
"	"		Weather cloudy with some showers. Wind S.W.	
"	15th	4.40a.m	Division report situation normal. 10 patrols went out.	Appx
"	"	4.40pm	Division report situation quiet.	Appx
"	"		Weather cloudy with heavy showers. Wind S.W.	Appx
"	16th	4.30am	Division report situation unchanged. Quiet night. Combined bombardment enemy trenches in A.16.d at 5pm. yesterday afternoon successful. Enemy retaliation slight.	Appx
"	"	4.38pm	Division report situation unchanged. Enemy 5.9" howitzers shelling two of our left group batteries all day with fullness observation. No serious damage.	Appx
"	"	7.47pm	180th Inf Bde report mine sprung by enemy at 7pm right centre of GRANGE S.2.2.C.2.0. Crater occupied with only slight opposition from snipers. Later enemy formed barrage W of crater. We appears to be 10 feet higher than their edge and consolidation now in progress. One casualty.	Appx

Army Form C. 2118

WAR DIARY
or
INTELLIGENCE SUMMARY
(Erase heading not required.)

Instructions regarding War Diaries and Intelligence Summaries are contained in F. S. Regs., Part II. and the Staff Manual respectively. Title Pages will be prepared in manuscript.

Place	Date	Hour	Summary of Events and Information	Remarks and references to Appendices
HERMAVILLE	16	7.58pm	Division report about nine to 17 Corps.	Capt
"	"		Weather fine. Wind S.W.	Capt
"	17	4.55am	Division report situation normal. Consolidation of new portion of Crater at S.22.C.20. proceeding satisfactorily. All quiet.	Capt
"	"	5pm	Division report situation quiet	Capt
"	"		Weather fine but cloudy. Heavy thunderstorm in afternoon + evening. Wind S.W.	Capt
"	18	4.47am	Division report situation quiet. Six patrols knocked out	Capt
"	"	4.45pm	Brigade report situation unchanged. At 3pm. our artillery in conjunction with 2"+ 3" TMs bombarded East side of WATLING STREET. Bombardment fell principally MONT ST ELOI shelled by 5.9" howitzer at 10am. Weather mostly mild + showery, then finer. Enemy 15 men in late afternoon and evening	Capt
"	19	4.45am	Brigade report situation normal. In reply to our bombardment of WATLING STREET enemy fired on our trenches O.63 and O.64 doing some damage with his artillery and T.M.s.	Capt
"	"	4.35pm	Division report situation quiet except for some hostile rifle grenade activity in our left sector with which our Stokes guns are dealing successfully. No shelling of back areas. Weather mostly in morning with heavy rain. Clearing till afternoon when it became fine. Wind N.W.	Capt
"	20	4.50am	Division report our artillery fired on enemy CTs at intervals throughout night no retaliation expected. In left sector enemy carried out a combined artillery + TM shoot against O.64 and O.65 at 9pm. doing some damage to our trenches but was quickly silenced by our artillery and T.M.s.	Capt
"	"	4.53pm	Division report quiet day. From 1.45pm. to 2.15pm. there was heavy firing by hostile guns onto right group batteries position. Wind N.W.	Capt
"	21	4.33am	Division report situation quiet. Hostile M.M. Heavy guns fired on battery position in F.5.d between 8 and 9pm without damage. Enemy T.M. active against O.63 knocking lift their camouflage. Our reply & defensive fire was	Capt
"	"	10.20am	Division report enemy Her camouflage in all Opposite to La Fauche C.T. at 6.5am. No morning. One missing officer 3 men	Capt

1875 Wt. W593/826 1,000,000 4/15 J.B.C. & A. A.D.S.S./Forms/C. 2118.

Army Form C. 2118

WAR DIARY
or
INTELLIGENCE SUMMARY
(Erase heading not required.)

Instructions regarding War Diaries and Intelligence Summaries are contained in F.S. Regs., Part II. and the Staff Manual respectively. Title Pages will be prepared in manuscript.

Place	Date	Hour	Summary of Events and Information	Remarks and references to Appendices
HERMAVILLE	21.	1:25pm	Division report further details of camouflet. No crater visible and very slight amount to our sap. Casualties caused by leakage of gas from explosion into a shaft whose entrance is in O68 resistance line. Casualties believed to be 10 off, 4 huncklings. 3 R.E.	GoC
"	"	5.10pm	Division report situation quiet.	
"	"	11.40pm	Division report we blew 2 camouflets in left sector at 7.30pm this evening one under left centre of GRANGE group, the other between GRANGE and DUFFIELD. Very little displacement of earth and little damage.	GoC
"	"		Weather fine. Wind N.W.	
"	22	4.38am	Division report situation normal. Left group batteries bombarded BROADMARSH CRATER at 5pm 21st in conjunction with Corps Heavy Artillery. Hostile artillery shelled CHASSERY during night doing slight damage.	GoC
"	"	4.38pm	Division report situation unchanged. Wind N.W.	GoC
"	"		Weather fine. Wind N.W.	GoC
"	23.	10pm	180th Inf Bde report two camouflets blown at 8pm by us, which demolished bank of 100 & 200 m between GRANGE and DUFFIELD craters. In consequence the from enemy position DUFFIELD uncovered. Sap leading to left front on GRANGE being deepened as enemy can now look into it.	Gop
"	23	4.37am	Division report situation normal. Our artillery retaliates guns fired on BROADMARSH at 7pm last night with good effect. Enemy reply weak. Wind N.W.	GoC
"	"	4.35am	Division report situation normal. Organised shoots on enemy back area dugouts at 5am & 6am by all 18pr batteries. Wind S.E.	GoC
"	"		Weather fine. Wind N.W. changing to S.E.	GoC
"	24	4.40am	Division report situation quiet. Our artillery fired salvoes at all suspected enemy dugouts at 7pm and 7.35pm.	GoC
"	"	4.45pm	Division report situation quiet. Our Stokes guns fired on enemy trenches between WATLING and LICHFIELD also on DEVON and DUFFIELD craters. Wind West.	GoC
"	"		Weather fine but cloudy. Wind W.	GoC

Army Form C. 2118

WAR DIARY
or
INTELLIGENCE SUMMARY
(Erase heading not required.)

Instructions regarding War Diaries and Intelligence Summaries are contained in F.S. Regs., Part II. and the Staff Manual respectively. Title Pages will be prepared in manuscript.

Place	Date	Hour	Summary of Events and Information	Remarks and references to Appendices
HERMAVILLE	25th	5.55am	Division report our left grp artillery bombarded WATLING CRATER at 5pm. A.A. at 11 pm. 2/18th London Regt raided enemy trenches in S 21 D. Trenches were found to be damaged badly and unoccupied. Whole party returned with one man slightly wounded.	G.K
"	"	4.47pm	Division report situation unchanged and quiet day. Wind S.W. Weather fair, cloudy with some heavy showers. Wind S.W.	G.K
"	26th	4.55am	2/14th Bn London Regt. Division report situation unchanged. Sentries patrols went out and carried out small enterprise on enemy's sap about A.16 central. No prisoners were taken and we suffered no casualties. Wind S.W.	G.K
"	"	4.47pm	Division report situation unchanged. Enemy howitzers shelled round GLASGOW dump and AUX RIETZ corner between 6.30 and 11 a.m. to-nite heavy. Weather cloudy with heavy showers. Wind S.W. & W.	G.K
"	27th	4.55am	Division report situation unchanged. Left sector report combined artillery and T.M. bombardment of DUFFIELD, DURAND took place. Enemy replied with artillery and T.M. damaging our trenches near GRANGE. Wind S.W.	G.K
"	"	4.55pm	Division report quiet day, wind S.W. wet + cloudy.	G.K
"	28th	4.55am	Division report quiet night. 16 patrols went out. Enemy post on BIRKIN was destroyed during the course of yesterday afternoon by our artillery and T.M.s. Enemy reply feeble. Wind S.W.	G.K
"	"	4.55pm	Division report situation quiet. Wind S.W. cloudy - sunny in morning + <s>fine afternoon + showers in evening</s> Fair in the afternoon + fine evening.	G.K
"	29th	4.30am	Division report situation normal. Raid carried out by 2/24 M.A. London Regt on craters opposite our right sector during the night. No Germans met.	G.K
"	"	10.50am	Division report all raiding party returned. One man slightly wounded. Party went beyond their objective. A 22 G 19.50 and Enfiled Bang Bip. No enemy were seen and there was no inhabitation until our	G.K
"	"		Recall signal was given when a few T.M. were fired.	G.K
"	"	4.45pm	Division report situation quiet. Heavy thunderstorm with afternoon. Wind N.E. Cloudy + sunny in the morning. Heavy thunderstorm with afternoon.	G.K

Army Form C. 2118

WAR DIARY
or
INTELLIGENCE SUMMARY
(Erase heading not required.)

Instructions regarding War Diaries and Intelligence Summaries are contained in F.S. Regs., Part II. and the Staff Manual respectively. Title Pages will be prepared in manuscript.

Place	Date	Hour	Summary of Events and Information	Remarks and references to Appendices
NERMAVILLE	30th	4.45am	Division report successful raid carried out at 2am by 2/19th Bn London Regt against enemy trenches of A 44 c 9 2 wounded and 6 unwounded prisoners were brought into our lines. Raiding party returned intact.	Apx
"	"	7.15am	G.O.C. sends congratulatory message to 180th Inf Bde and 2/19th Ld R. on success of raid	Apx
"	"	11.45am	Army Commander congratulates Gen BULFIN and all concerned on success of raid last night	Apx
"	"	12.10pm	Army Commanders message sent to 180th Inf Bde.	Apx
"	"	4.55pm	Division report situation quiet	Apx
"	"		Weather very wet. Heavy rain & westerly gale blowing all day	Apx
"	31st	4.37am	Division report quiet night. Nothing unusual to report.	Apx
"	"	4.54pm	Division report situation normal. Quiet day. Wind N.W.	Apx
"	"	5.20pm	Division report enemy flew canon fet 3.15pm En.ob of GRANGE. K mine shaft slightly damaged. Rescue party getting to work. No change in	Apx
"	"		Two men brought up gassed one man cut off.	Apx
"	"		Surface. Weather fine. Wind N.W.	

31.8.1916

Addison Captain
Gen Staff
60th Division

SECRET.

Vol 4

War Diary.

General Staff, 60th (London) Division.

From. 1st September 1916

To. 30th September 1916.

Army Form C. 2118

WAR DIARY
or
INTELLIGENCE SUMMARY
(Erase heading not required.)

Instructions regarding War Diaries and Intelligence Summaries are contained in F.S. Regs., Part II. and the Staff Manual respectively. Title Pages will be prepared in manuscript.

Place	Date	Hour	Summary of Events and Information	Remarks and references to Appendices
HERMAVILLE.	1st	4.45am	Division report left sector report our artillery and T.M.'s bombarded WATLING CRATER 6.20pm damaging enemy's trenches and sap leading to Crater. Working party was seen to be repairing the sap at the time. Situation otherwise normal.	Enc
"	"	5.2pm	Division report about 20 shells were fired into ETRUN between 1.15pm and 2.15pm. There were apparently fired by naval gun direction south by west. Barracks at A2a 55.42 heavily shelled with about 100 shells commencing 11pm. 45 of these were blind. Wind S.W. Weather fine. Wind S.W.	Encl
"	2nd	4.40am	Division report situation unchanged. Wind S.W.	Encl
"	"	4.54pm	Division report enemy active with T.M.'s in O.63 and P.93. These are being dealt with. Situation otherwise normal. Weather fine. Wind S.E & E.	Encl
"	3rd	4.35am	Division report situation quiet. Nothing to report.	Encl
"	"	4.52pm	Division report quiet day. Nothing unusual to report. Wind S.W. Weather fine but in the morning. Heavy rainy in evening. Wind S.W. Lewis of bombardment in the south heard all day.	Encl
"	4th	5am	Division report quiet night situation unchanged. Attempted raid by 2/22nd Bn on enemy trenches at A.22.a.9.9. failed owing to wire. Many patrols were out.	Encl
"	"	4.55pm	Division report quiet day situation unchanged.	Encl (S28.a.40.35.)
"	"	5.55pm	Left sector report camouflet blown at 5.10pm by enemy between COMMON and VERNON Craters. Surface of ground not broken. No casualties and no damage to our posts or saps.	Encl
"	"		Most day with continuous frequent storms. Wind W.	Encl
"	5th	4.3am	Division report situation quiet. Wind S.W.	Encl
"	"	4.45pm	Division report situation unchanged. Nothing unusual to report. Wet day. Wind S.W.	Encl

1875 Wt. W593/826 1,000,000 4/15 J.B.C. & A. A.D.S.S./Forms/C. 2118.

Army Form C. 2118

WAR DIARY
or
INTELLIGENCE SUMMARY
(Erase heading not required.)

Instructions regarding War Diaries and Intelligence Summaries are contained in F. S. Regs., Part II. and the Staff Manual respectively. Title Pages will be prepared in manuscript.

Place	Date	Hour	Summary of Events and Information	Remarks and references to Appendices
HERMEVILLE	6th	4.35am	Division report situation unchanged.	Gnl
"	"	4.53pm	Division report situation quiet. Artillery active for bombardment enemy trenches is being carried out with apparently successful results - wind N.E.	Gnl
"	"		Weather fine. Wind N.E. to E.	Gnl
"	"	11.35pm	Division report enemy exploded mine about A.10.6.9.0.30. at 10.15 pm.	Gnl
"	7th	12.15am	Division report casualties from mine small. Artillery ceased fire 10.54 pm	Gnl
"	"	54?am	Division report casualties were 3 killed & 12 wounded. Enemy did not leave his trenches and Consolidation well in hand. Many patrols out. Wind S to North. The guns ceased fire at 10.54 pm	Gnl
"	"	10.40am	Division report enemy flare camouflet about A.16.a. 9.8. this morning at 6.30 am. No casualties & no damage to galleries. Surface not broken.	Gnl
"	"	5.12pm	Division report we exploded a mine at A.10.b. 30.35 at 3.10pm. which formed small crater. A combined artillery and T.M. bombardment of ALBANY crater was carried out beginning at 12 noon today. Wind N.E.	Gnl
"	"	6.30/pm	Division report enemy shelled NEUVILLE ST VAAST keenly between 3.30 and 4.30 pm with 5.9 + 4.2.	Gnl
"	"		Weather fine. Wind N.E.	Gnl
"	8th	4.35am	Division report situation normal. Our Artillery bombardment on R.J. Crater in progress. Wind N.E.	Gnl
"	"	4.53pm	Division report situation quiet. Artillery normal. Wind N.E.	Gnl
"	"		Weather fine. Wind N.E.	Gnl
"	9th	4.30am	Division report situation unchanged. We carried out an artillery bombardment between 6.30 pm and 1.30 am to be for with suspected enemy relief. Numerous patrols were out.	Gnl
"	"	4.45pm	Division report situation unchanged. Artillery carrying out hot concentrations. Wind N.E.	Gnl
"	"		Weather fine. Misty in morning. Wind	Gnl

WAR DIARY or INTELLIGENCE SUMMARY

Army Form C. 2118

Place	Date	Hour	Summary of Events and Information	Remarks and references to Appendices
HERMAVILLE	10	4.45am	Division report situation unchanged. Many patrols out bound N.E.	
"	"	4.40pm	Division report situation quiet. Very hazy bound N.E. Weather fine. Misty in morning. Division conds unfer 1st Army from 12 noon.	
"	11	4.30am	Division reports two very successful raids carried out. At S.21d.92.75 three of four prisoners belonging to 122nd Regiment were taken. Our losses 2 men wounded and 3 missing. At A.16a.95.35 four unwounded and one wounded prisoners were taken belonging to 184th Regiment. All returned, six wounded. Raid at S.21d.92.75 carried out at 3am by 2/20th Ln.R. and raid at A.16a.95.35 at 3am by 2/15th Bn Ln.R.	
"	"	6.30am	Division report four prisoners taken at S.21.d.92.75 and four were not five at A.16.a.95.35 report four prisoners taken were Battalions or divisions of raid.	
"	"	8.37am	G.O.C. Division sends congratulations to both Battalions on success of raid.	
"	"	1.30pm	Army Commander sends congratulations All concerned on success of raid, and message to be passed to all dec. units.	
"	"	5.2pm	Division report situation normal. Centre Group report 20 yards of wire cut from N.W.	
"	"	5.40pm	Portion of trenches on extreme left from CENTRAL AVE to LASALLE AVE (exc) handed over to 9th Div. Weather fine bound N.W.	
"	12	4.30am	Division report situation unchanged.	
"	"	4.50pm	Division report situation unchanged. Aeroplane fire generally. Some shrapnel bound N.W.	
"	13	4.30am	Division report situation unchanged.	
"	"	4.40pm	Division report situation quiet. Artillery carried out some shelling. Weather fine bound N.W.	

Army Form C. 2118

WAR DIARY
or
INTELLIGENCE SUMMARY
(Erase heading not required.)

Instructions regarding War Diaries and Intelligence Summaries are contained in F. S. Regs., Part II. and the Staff Manual respectively. Title Pages will be prepared in manuscript.

Place	Date	Hour	Summary of Events and Information	Remarks and references to Appendices
HERMAVILLE	14.	4.30 am	Division report situation unchanged.	Cal
"	"	1.20 pm	Division report enemy flew a mine at 7 am at A16 a 75.25. It could not be discovered where it was. Moon for 3 hours. It is now observed to have made a long low crater. There were no casualties.	Cal
"	"	4.45 pm	Division report situation unchanged. Weather fine. Wind N.W.	Cal
"	15.	4.25 am	Division report situation unchanged. Wind light N.W.	Cal
"	"	4.30 pm	Division report situation unchanged. Centre Group artillery cut some 30 yards wire. Wind N.W.	Cal
"	16	4.55 am	Division report situation unchanged. Fletsen patrols out during night. Wind N.W.	Cal
"	"	4.45 pm	Division report situation unchanged. Weather fine. Wind N.W. slight.	Cal
"	17	4.55 am	Division report situation normal. Several patrols went out. Artillery cut wire at A4 a 85.10. and S21.c.95.60.	Cal
"	"	4.40 pm	Division report situation unchanged. Weather fine. Wind N.W. very slight.	Cal
"	18	4.25 am	Division report situation unchanged. During yesterday we cut about 150 yards of his wire in our left sector.	Cal
"	"	4.40 pm	Division report situation quiet day. Wind N.W. Very wet day. Fair evening. Wind slight N.W.	Cal
"	19	4.50 am	Division report situation unchanged. Numerous patrols were out. Nothing to report.	Cal
"	"	4.50 pm	Division report situation normal. Wind N.N.E. Weather fair with heavy showers.	Cal

WAR DIARY
or
INTELLIGENCE SUMMARY
(Erase heading not required.)

Army Form C. 2118

Instructions regarding War Diaries and Intelligence Summaries are contained in F.S. Regs., Part II. and the Staff Manual respectively. Title Pages will be prepared in manuscript.

Place	Date	Hour	Summary of Events and Information	Remarks and references to Appendices
HERMAVILLE	20	4.25am	Division report situation unchanged. Our artillery cut about 50 yds wire.	CMS
"	"	4.40pm	Division report situation quiet.	CMS
"	"		Weather dull with heavy showers. Wind NW gusty.	CMS
"	21.	5.55am	Division report raid attempted at 3am last by 2/24th Bn. Quite unsuccessful. All party returned. Observe situation quiet. Wind NNE.	CMS
"	"	4.45pm	Division report situation quiet. Wind NNE.	CMS
"	"	7.7pm	Division report mine blown by us at 6.29½pm about S.22.c.15.18. It has formed straight a ridge between DUFFIELD and GRANGE. German activities on DUFFIELD and GRANGE at 6.34pm. Wind NNE. Weather fair.	CMS
"	22	4.35am	Division report. At 6.30pm we blew craters at S.22.c.1.2. Our lip is being consolidated. A raid was attempted on the enemy trenches at A.16.c.7.4. but failed to get into the hostile trenches owing to rifle fire. All the party has returned. Situation otherwise quiet.	CMS CMS
"	"	4.35pm	Division report quiet day. Wind NNE.	CMS
"	"		10.4am Other fire wind NNG.	CMS
"	23.	4.25am	Division report situation quiet.	CMS
"	"	4.35pm	Division report situation quiet. Weather fine. Wind SSE.	CMS CMS
"	24.	12.10am	Division report raid on enemy trenches between A.4.d.37.06 and A.4.d.40.26 successful, all raiding party back. 5 prisoners taken of whom one wounded all of 104th Inf. Regt. by 2/18th Bn.	CMS
"	"	12.20am	Division report raid by 2/13th Bn on A.22.b.8.3. failed to enter enemy trenches and was repulsed by bomb and rifle. One officer missing.	CMS
"	"	4.40am	Division report reports about raid stating casualties in second raid 1 off. 1 Sgt. killed 4 men wounded. Situation otherwise quiet and 40 yards of wire cut by artillery.	CMS
"	"	8 A.m.	Corps Commander 17th Corps were congratulations to centre Brigade (179th) and 2/16 & 2/18 Bn Lond R.	CMS
"	"	9.55am	G.O.C. Division was Congratulations to 2/16th Bn. Lond. R.	CMS

Army Form C. 2118

WAR DIARY
or
INTELLIGENCE SUMMARY
(Erase heading not required.)

Instructions regarding War Diaries and Intelligence Summaries are contained in F.S. Regs., Part II. and the Staff Manual respectively. Title Pages will be prepared in manuscript.

Place	Date	Hour	Summary of Events and Information	Remarks and references to Appendices
HERMAVILLE	24	4:34pm	Division report situation quiet. Artillery bombarded Crater posts and T.M. positions in neighbourhood of ARGYLL craters between 11 am and 6pm	ad
"	"		Weather fine. Wind S & S.W.	Cal
"	25.	4.40am	Division report situation unchanged. Numerous patrols were out.	Cal
"	"	4:34pm	Division report quiet day. Nothing to report. Wind S.E.	Fd
"	"		Weather fine. Wind S.E.	and
"	26	1·5am	Division report camouflet blown by us in left sector at 11.15pm yesterday at A4 a 63.68. No damage reported to our posts	Cd
"	"	4.35am	Division report situation unchanged.	Cd
"	"	4·30pm	Division report situation very quiet.	and
"	"		Weather fine. Wind SE & E.	Cd
"	27.	4·25am	Division report situation quiet. Several patrols went out. Wind S.E.	Cd
"	"	4·40pm	Division report considerable hostile TM activity on left. 1 Subsector. Our firing line damaged in several places. Otherwise quiet.	and
"	"		Weather fine with one or two showers. Wind strong S.E.	Cd
"	28	4·25am	Division report situation quiet.	Cd
"	"	4·40pm	Division report situation unchanged. Wind S.E.	Cd
"	"		Weather fine after early showers.	Cd
"	29	4:35am	Division report situation unchanged. Twelve patrols were out.	Cd
"	"	4·25pm	Division report situation unchanged. Hostile machine gun & T.M. fired intermittently on left. One subsector during morning and afternoon doing some damage. Wind N.E.	and
"	"		Weather fine mostly & dull with one or two showers. Wind N.E.	Cd
"	30.	4.3.15am	Division report raid on enemy trenches at A16 a 95.95 successful. 5 prisoners 107th R. Regt captured. All party back. One man killed two wounded.	and

Army Form C. 2118

WAR DIARY
or
INTELLIGENCE SUMMARY
(Erase heading not required.)

Place	Date	Hour	Summary of Events and Information	Remarks and references to Appendices
HERMAVILLE	30	4.25am	Division report situation unchanged. Wind N.W.	Apx
"	"	9.7am	G.O.C. Division wires congratulations to 2/14th T.B.A. on success of raid.	Apx
"	"	9.30am	Corps Commander wires congratulations to 17th T.M. Bty & 2/14th T.B.A.	Apx
"	"	11.45am	Division report our Casualties in raid now amount to 1 killed, Six wounded, two missing.	Apx
"	"	4.30pm	Division report hostile medium TM's active during the morning in left sector. Three enemy aeroplanes flew over the left sector lines between 8am and 10 am at a height of 200 feet. Wind N.E. Weather fine. Wind N.W.	Apx

30.9.1916

A.R. Wilson Tyslaw Col.
60th Division

WAR DIARY

SECRET.　　　　　　　　　　　　　　　　　　　　　　　　　　Copy No.......

60th DIVISION.

DEFENCE SCHEME.

1. The Front line to be held by this Division extends from the point where the avenue Ab del Kader cuts the front line N. of Roclincourt (exc.) to the Avenue Central (exc.). (Trenches L.20 - P.79, both inc.).

    The 21st Division is on the Right and the 9th Division on the Left of the Divisional Line.

    The Southern Boundary of the Division is:-　　Ab del Kader Ave.(exc) - Filatiers Ave.(exc) up to where it cuts the LILLE Road - Road from G.3. Central to Bridge over River Scarpe at G.8.c.3.7. (Road & Bridge exc.).
    The Northern boundary of the Division is Central Ave. (exc).

2. The Line is organised for defence as follows:-

    (a). Front Line system which is subdivided into:-
    　(i). Observation Line, which consists of advanced posts on craters or in sap-heads.
    　(ii). Firing Line: A continuous line immediately in rear of the observation line. This is the main line of resistance and is to be held to the last.
    　(iii). Support Line: A line immediately in rear of the firing line at a distance varying from 80 to 100 yds., provided with strong points.
    　(iv). Reserve Line: Including the fortified post of Ecurie, Labyrinthe Redoubt, Work A, Work B, Fork Redoubt, Elbe Trench, Neuville St. Vaast, Palace and Empire. This line is supported by the work at Maison Blanche.

    (b). Corps Line running from St. Aubin Northwards and passing just E. of Berthonval Wood.

    (c). Army Line running N. and S. just E. of Haute Avesnes.

3. **Delimitation of Sectors.**
    The line is divided into three sectors as per attached map. Sector Commanders are responsible for the defence and up-keep of areas as shown. They have no responsibility as regards Corps and Army lines.

    The Front Lines and Main Communication Trenches are as follows:-
    Right Sector:
    　From the Avenue Ab del Kader (Trench L.20) to Trench M.33 (both inc.)
    　C.T's: Genie, Anzin and Aniversaire Avenues.

    Centre Sector:
    　From Trench M.34 to where Trench O.61 cuts Lichfield Ave. (both inc.).
    　C.T's: Vase, Sapour and Territorial Avenues.

    Left Sector:
    　From where Trench O.61 cuts Lichfield Ave.(exc.) to Trench P.79 (inc.).
    　C.T's: Denis le Rook and Pont St.

4. **Distribution of Troops.**
    (i) Right Sector:
    　181 Inf. Bde.　　　　　　　　　H.Q.　　　　Etrun.
    　　　　　　　　　　Adv.　　　　H.Q.　　　　A.27.a.6.1
    　　　　　Div. Reserve　　　　　Bn.　　　　 Etrun.
    　Right Art. Group.　　　　　　H.Q.　　　　G.9.b.2.9.
    　3/3 Fd. Co. R.E.　　　　　　 H.Q.　　　　Anzin
    　1 Co. Pioneer Bn.　　　　　　　　　　　　 Ecurie.

-2-

(ii) Centre Sector.
179 Inf. Bde.   H.Q.   Ecoivres.
                            Adv. H.Q.   A.8.d.2.5.
        Div. Reserve Bn.   Bray.
Centre Art. Group.   H.Q.   Vase Avenue.A.19.c.5.3.
2/4 Fd. Co. R.E.   H.Q.   A.8.d.
1 Co. Pioneer Bn. and   Maison Blanche.
    4 Lewis guns.

(iii) Left Sector.
180 Inf. Bde.   H.Q.   Mont St. Eloy.
                            Adv. H.Q.   A.8.c.7.9.
        Div. Reserve Bn.   Mont St. Eloy.
Left Art. Group.   H.Q.   Berthonval Fm.
1/6 Fd. Co. R.E.   H.Q.   A.8.a.2.2.
1 Co. Pioneer Bn. and   Neuville St. Vaast.
    3 Lewis guns.

The Reserve Bn. in each Sector will form the Divisional Reserve.

5. **Communications.**

(a) The following telephonic communications exist :-

Cos. in Front Line with Bn. H.Q., with Cos. on their flanks and, through F.O.Os, to the Battery covering their front.
Bn. H.Q. with Bde. H.Q. and Bns. on their flanks.
Bde. H.Q. with Div. H.Q. and with the Artillery Group allotted to their Sector.
Art. Groups with C.R.A. to whom they should apply for the co-operation of the Heavy Artillery.

6. **Action in case of Attack.**

In the event of a serious attack, the following arrangements will be carried out :-

(a) **Staffs.**

Adv. H.Q. will be established as follows :-
Div. H.Q. at Etrun, with command post at Brunehaut Farm.
Sector Commanders to the places named in para. 4.

(b) **Sectors.**

In case of a heavy bombardment, the firing line will not be reinforced. All troops in the lines which are being shelled should take cover in dug-outs, etc., with the exception of sentries and 2 men per Lewis or Machine Gun, until the alarm is given that the enemy is advancing.

Companies will be sent up from Divisional Reserve as follows :-

1 Co. from Bn. at Etrun for reinforcement of Ecurie, under orders from Right Sector Commander.
1 Co. from Bn at Bray for reinforcement of "B"Work, Fork Redoubt and Elbe trench, under orders from Centre Sector Commander.
1 Co. from Bn at Mont St. Eloy for reinforcement of Neuville St. Vaast and occupation of Palace and Empire Works, under orders from Left Sector Commander.

Sector Commanders must make arrangements for meeting all forms of attack, and will ensure that Commanders of all strong points know their duties.

Should the enemy succeed in penetrating any part of our line, a counter-attack is to be organised at once to eject him.

This counter-attack should, as a rule, be organised by the commander on the spot, so that it may be carried out rapidly and thus deny to the enemy the necessary time to consolidate the position he has won. Counter-attacking troops should invariably have strong parties of bombers. The penetration of any one portion of the line is on no account to be taken as a reason for withdrawal from any other portion which has not been penetrated.

The minimum garrisons of fortified posts in the Reserve Line, viz., Ecurie, Maison Blanche and Neuville St. Vaast, etc., etc., are on no account to be employed in counter-attacks.

The Bns. in Div. Reserve will assemble on their alarm posts, but will not be moved (except the Cos. mentioned above) without authority from Div. H.Q.

(c) Pioneers.

The O.C., Pioneer Bn. will send up the resting platoons of his Bn. from Louez to reinforce the garrison at Maison Blanche.

The O.C., Pioneer Bn. will assume command of this garrison.

Companies allotted to the various sectors will act under the orders of the Sector Commanders. Their general role should be as part of the garrisons of the strong points in the sectors in which they are working.

(d) R.E.

The Field and Tunnelling Cos. will Stand to Arms in their billets. Detachments working in the trenches will act under the orders of the Commander of the Sector in which they are working.

(e) Warning.

A priority message "ATTACK QUARTERS" will be sent when necessary to bring the whole of this scheme into operation, but Sector Commanders may bring that portion of it affecting their Sector into operation where they consider the circumstances require it, reporting their action to Div. H.Q.

(f) Gas Alarm.

See Appendix "F".

7. Defence of Second Line.

In the event of a withdrawal to the Corps Line being ordered, Sector Commanders will be responsible for holding the portion of that line which falls within their area.

8. Mining Fatigues.

(a) Those not actually at work at the shafts will be at the disposal of the Sector Commander in whose area they are billetted, e.g. Those billetted in Aux Rietz and Neuville St. Vaast will be at the disposal of the Left Sector Commander. Those in Maroeuil are to form part of the Div. Reserve.

(b) Those actually working at the shafts will be at the disposal of the Sector Commander in whose area they are working. The general principle on which these units should be employed is that they should be allotted special fire bays which they would man under the command of their own officers.

9. The following appendices are attached:-

    (a) Destination of troops in Div. Reserve (if ordered), Routes to the same and times required to reach destination. Instructions for Bn.. Commanders in Div. Reserve.

    (b) Battle Straggler Posts and Custody of Prisoners.

    (c) Garrisons of defended localities and instructions regarding the same.

    (d) "S.O.S." messages.

    (e) Artillery co-operation with Corps Heavy Artillery and neighbouring Divisions.

    (f) Action on receipt of "GAS ALERT".

    (g) Medical arrangements.

    (h) Map.

25/8/16.

Lt. Col.
General Staff.

APPENDIX "A".

MOVEMENTS OF TROOPS IN DIVISIONAL RESERVE TO POSITIONS OF ASSEMBLY.

UNIT.	FROM.	TO.	ROUTE.	TIME REQUIRED TO REACH DESTINATION.	REMARKS.
(1) 1 Co. 181 Inf. Bde.	Etrun.	Ecurie.	Anzin Avenue.	1¼ hours.	No larger bodies of troops than a platoon are to march together. Intervals between platoons should be about 5 minutes.
(2) 1 Bn. 181 Inf. Bde. (less 1 Co.)	Etrun.	Corps Line Trenches N. of St. Aubin.	Anzin Road.	1 hour.	
(3) Details, Pioneer Bn.	Louez.	Maison Blanche.	Sapper or Vase Avenue.	1½ hours.	
(4) 1 Bn. 179 Inf. Bde. (less 1 Co.)	Bray.	Group of old works just W. of Maison Blanche (Moissonouse).	Maroeuil, Sapper or Vase Avenues.	2 hours.	
(5) 1 Co. 179 Inf. Bde.	Bray.	"B" Fort and Elbe Trench.	Maroeuil, Sapper, Claudot or Territorial Avenues.	2½ hours.	
(6) 1 Bn. 180 Inf. Bde. (less 1 Co.)	Mont St. Eloy.	Fort George & Corps Line N. & S. of Fort George.	Pont Street or Chaussery, Ecoivres Avenues.	1½ hours.	
(7) 1 Co. 180 Inf. Bde.	Mont St. Eloy.	Nouville St. Vaast.	Denis le Rock or Tramway.	2 hours.	

P.T.O.

1.   The probable moves of Bns. in Div. Reserve are shown overleaf. Each O.C., Bn. will detail 4 officers and 4 N.C.Os. when their Bn. is in Divisional Reserve, to reconnoitre the routes laid down, so that guides will be available to lead the Bn. to its destination.

2.   Should it be necessary to concentrate the whole of the Div. Reserve, it will be commanded by the Senior Bn. Commander of the Bns. in Div. Reserve.   The G.S.O.3. will act as his Staff Officer.

The most probable place of concentration would be in the neighbourhood of Maison Blanche and those Bns. of the Right and Left Sector, in Div. Reserve, in addition to reconnoitring the routes mentioned in para. (1) above, will also detail 4 officers and 4 N.C.Os. to reconnoitre the routes to Maison Blanche from Etrun and Mont St. Eloy respectively.

APPENDIX "B".

BATTLE STRAGGLER POSTS - CUSTODY OF PRISONERS.

In the case of active operations :-

1. Battle Straggler Posts will be organised in the Division as follows :-

    (a). BRIGADE POSTS.

    Posts will be established under Brigade arrangements along the Bethune - Arras Road.

    Should the Divisional Front be broken, these Posts will re-assemble on the line of the Divisional Posts as follows :-

    Louez - Maroeuil - Bray - Mont St. Eloy.

    (b). DIVISIONAL POSTS.

    Posts will be placed at the following points :-

    Reference Map 51c. 1/40,000.

    L.8.b.3.9.
    L.9.b.2.7.
    L.4.a.5.6.
    F.28.c.5.5.
    F.28.a.2.9.
    F.15.d.8.1.
    F.9.c.10.00
    F.9.a.5.4.
    F.9.a.00.10.

    COLLECTING STATIONS.

    To which unwounded stragglers will be conducted will be formed at the headquarters of the Bns. in Div. Reserve, and will be under the Quartermaters of those Bns.   They will be sent back to their Units from here under an officer or N.C.O.

2. PRISONERS.

    Prisoners will be taken over from Inf. Bdes. under Corps arrangements at Anzin Church, Maroeuil Church and Bray Huts.

APPENDIX "O".

DEFENDED LOCALITIES.

Name of Work.	Garrison Permanent.	Garrison Maximum.	Machine Guns.	Lewis Rifles.	S.A.A.	Reserve Grenades.	Reserve Rations.	Remarks.
Ecurie.	1½ Cos.	5 Cos.	2.	6.	252000.	1500.	2 days.	
Labyrinthe.	"	2 Sections.	"	1.	"	"	"	
A. Work.	"	1 Platoon.	"	1.	10000.	120.	2 days.	
B. Work.	"	2 Platoons.	"	1.	10000.	120.	"	
Fork Redoubt and Sapper Shelters.	1 Co.	2 Cos.	2.	"	16000.	4700.	from Maison Blanche.	
Bertata.	1 Platoon.	2 Platoons.	1.	"	20000.	240.	2 days.	
Zivy.	1 Platoon.	2 Platoons.	1.	"	20000.	240.	"	
Maison Blanche.	1 Co.	2 Cos.	4.	6.	252000.	750.	"	
Neuville St. Vaast.	1 Bn.	2 Bns.	6.	8.	294000.	3000.	"	
Empire.	"	2 Platoons.	1.	3	18000.	180.		Under construction.

1.	The following strong points must, in the event of attack, have minimum garrisons as under :-

(i.) <u>Ecurie and Ferme des Caves.</u>   1 Co. and 3 platoons; 6 Lewis or Machine Guns.   The O.C., Pioneer Co. will act as Staff Officer to the Officer detailed to command this garrison.   Two platoons of the Pioneer Co. should occupy the Sausage Redoubt and the remainder of the garrison be distributed along the Northern, Eastern and South-Eastern faces of Ecurie proper.   Should the Co. mentioned in para. 6. defence scheme be ordered up, it should remain in the Rocade Avenue, where it will be available for reinforcing the Ecurie Garrison.

(ii) <u>LABYRINTHE REDOUBT.</u>   2 Sections and 1 Lewis Gun under an officer.   These troops should be detailed either from that Co. of the 181 Inf. Bde. which is in Ecurie or from the Co. in the Sunken road A.21.b.0.7.

(iii) <u>B. Fort.</u>   1 platoon and 2 Lewis or Machine Guns.

(iv) <u>Fork Redoubt and Elbe Trench.</u>   3 platoons and 2 Lewis or Machine Guns.

(v) <u>Neuville St. Vaast.</u>   The Pioneer Co. working in the Left Sector and the troops composing the Mining Fatigue will form the garrison of this village. The Co. mentioned in para. 6. of defence scheme will come up in support, if ordered by Left Sector Commander.   8 Lewis or Machine Guns will also be allotted to this village. The Town Major will act as Staff Officer to the officer detailed to command this village.

(vi) <u>Palace and Empire.</u>   1 platoon is to be allotted between these two works.

2.	Those of the above works which are permanently occupied will be manned once during the tour of duty of the troops occupying them.

	In the case of Neuville St. Vaast where owing to Mining Fatigues it is not possible to fully man the work at the same time, all Officers and Senior N.C.Os. must be fully acquainted with the portion of the work which they will be called upon to defend.

3.	Orders for the occupation of Ecurie and Neuville St. Vaast are to be made out by the Sector Commander in whose area these places lie. These orders must contain the detail of allotment of troops to their various places in the work.

SECRET.   INSTRUCTIONS FOR "S.O.S."   APPENDIX "D"

1. All previous regulations for the "S.O.S." message are cancelled and the following will be substituted.

2. The "S.O.S." message is only to be used in extreme urgency. It denotes that certain portions of our lines have been or are about to be attacked.

3. The "S.O.S." message will be sent by telephone followed by the trench call of the Sector or Sub-sector in question. In the event of failure of the telephone system, rockets will be used. The recognised trench calls are, "Right", "Centre", "Left", or "Right One", "Right Two", "Centre One", "Centre Two", "Left One", "Left Two".
    The rocket signal for the "S.O.S." will be :-
    Three green rockets fired in quick succession.
    The above signal is to be repeated until the artillery has opened fire.

    In the event of an explosion of a mine by the enemy, all Batteries of the Group covering the Sector in which the mine explodes, will stand to their guns. Fire will be opened only on the request of the Infantry Commander on the spot or F.O.O. by telephone or rocket, and will be controlled by the F.O.O. in consultation with the Infantry Commander.

4. On receipt of the "S.O.S." message or signal, the field guns and Howitzers immediately supporting the portion of the line attacked, also the Batteries covering the portion on either flank, will at once open fire on their "Night" or "Barrage" Lines.
    40 rounds per field gun and Howitzer will be fired at a rapid rate of fire, after which section fire, 15 seconds for 18-pdrs. and section fire 30 seconds for 4.5 Howitzers will be maintained until further information is received.
    In order to avoid useless expenditure of ammunition this fire should be stopped as soon as it is known that no further danger exists, even before the 40 rounds per gun have been fired. This order to cease fire will be sent by telephone by the F.O.O. after consultation with the Infantry Commander. Rockets are NOT to be used for this purpose.

5. The Battery who first receives the "S.O.S." will transmit it to the Group Commander, who will order Batteries to open fire in accordance with para. 4 above, if they have not already done so.

6. If the Infantry Brigade Commander wishes all Batteries of the Group to open fire at the same time for the "S.O.S." he will himself send the "S.O.S." viz.: "S.O.S.Right", "S.O.S.Centre", "S.O.S.Left", according to his "trench call", direct to the Group Commander.
    On receipt of this message by the Group Commander from the Infantry Brigade Commander all Batteries of the Group will open fire as in para. 4.
    If the assistance of Heavy Artillery is required, application must be made to Divisional Headquarters for the same. Similarly, application must be made to Divisional Headquarters for the assistance of the Artillery of Divisions on either flank, if required.

7. The scheme will be tested periodically in accordance with Divisional Standing Orders, page 24.
    A Staff Officer will hand to an Infantry Commander or to an F.O.O. the message "TEST BATTERY".
    On receipt of this message, the Infantry Officer or the F.O.O. will at once transmit the message to the Battery covering his front. The Battery will fire one round.
    The time will be taken by the Staff Officer from the time of the delivery of the message by him to the time when this round is fired.

8. Rockets are NOT to be fired except to commence the "S.O.S."

                                            E. T. Humphreys.
                                            Lieut-Colonel,
                                            General Staff.

H.Q., 60th Div.,
29th Sept, 1916.

APPENDIX "E.2."

SUPPORT OF XVII CORPS BY IV CORPS.

(a) **SITUATION.** Minor attack on XVII Corps Left.

SIGNAL. "Barrage 'P' Sector."

SENT BY Left Group 60th Division to Right Group ~~9th~~ Right Division.

ACTION TAKEN BY ~~9th~~ Right Divisional Artillery.

Group.	Battery.	Target.
	1 18-pr. Batty.	Barrage Trench S.21.b.50.25. to S.21.d.70.80.
	1 18-pr. Batty.	Barrage Trench S.21.d.70.80. to S.21.d.95.85.
	1 Section 4.5" Hows.	Trench Junction. S.22.c.30.45.
	1 gun 4.5" How.	Trench Junction. S.22.c.27.78.
	1 gun 4.5" How.	Trench Junction. S.22.a.20.00.

(b) **SITUATION.** Serious attack on XVII Corps left.

SIGNAL. "Defend 60th Division Left".

SENT BY 60th Division to ~~9th~~ Right Division.

ACTION TAKEN BY ~~9th~~ Right Divisional Artillery.

Group.	Battery.	Target.
	1 18-pr. Batty.	Enfilade C.T. (COMMUNE). S.22.c.3.7. to S.22.d.5.5.
	1 18-pr. Batty.	Barrage Trenches and BROADMARSH CRATER system in S.21.d.
	1 Section 4.5" Hows.	Block C.T. Junction at S.23.c.1.4½.
	1 Section 4.5" Hows.	Block C.T. Junctions at S.23.c.4.3.
	1, 2, or more 18-pr. Batteries and 1 4.5" How. Battery.	Available if they can be spared after having run guns out of emplacements to reinforce 60th Divisional Artillery fire as situation develops and as requested by 60th Division.

APPENDIX "E.1."

ARTILLERY CO-OPERATION.

SUPPORT OF IV CORPS BY XVII CORPS.

(a). SITUATION. Minor Attack on IV Corps right flank.
SIGNAL. "Barrage 'Q' Sector".
SENT BY. Right Group 9th Division to Left Group 60th Division.
ACTION TAKEN BY 60th Divisional Artillery.

Group.	Battery.	Target.
Left.	1 18-pr. Batty.	Barrage Trench S.21.b.50.25. to S.21.d.70.90.
	1 18-pr. Batty.	Barrage Trench S.21.d.70.80. to S.21.d.95.85.
	1 Section 4.5" How.	Enfilade C.T. S.21.d.95.85. to S.22.a.10.50.
	1 Section 4.5" How.	Enfilade C.T. S.21.d.70.80. to S.21.b.70.30.
Centre.	No action, but "stand by" ready to barrage on Left Group front.	

(b). SITUATION. Serious attack on IV Corps Right.
SIGNAL. "Defend Right Division Right".
SENT BY. Right 9th Division to 60th Division.
ACTION TAKEN BY 60th Divisional Artillery.

Group.	Battery.	Co-ordinates of positions.	Target.	Remarks.
Left.	1 18-pr. Batty.	F.5.b.3.8.	Enfilade Sunken Road. S.16.c.6.5. to S.16.b.0.5.	All immediately available, provided 60th Divnl. Front not threatened.
	1 18-pr. Batty.	A.7.d.8.2½.	Enfilade C.T. S.22.a.1½.6. to S.22.a.9.9.	
	1 4.5" How.Batty.	S.25.b.2½.1.	BROADMARSH Crater system, S.21.d.8.8.	
	Single 15 pr. Gun.	A.3.b.3.5.	Enfilade trenches in S.21.b. and d.	
R.H.A.	Single 18-pr. Gun.	A.15.d.1.8.	Enfilade trenches in S.21.b. and d.	
Left.	1 4.5" How.Batty.	F.18.a.0.0.	Pull out ready to reinforce Right 9th Division; fire in Squares S.15. or S.14. as the situation develops and as ordered by Right 9th Division.	Available if they can be spared after having run guns out of emplacements to prepared sites in the open.
	1 18-pr. Batty.	F.5.d.4.6.		
	1 18-pr. Batty.	F.18.c.2.2½.		
Centre.	1 18-pr. Batty.	F.24.c.5.5.		
	Remaining Batteries.		Stand by ready to barrage on Left Group Front.	

APPENDIX E.1.

DIVISIONAL ARTILLERY.

SUPPORT OF IV CORPS BY XVII CORPS.

(a).   SITUATION:-   Minor Attack on IV Corps right flank.
       SIGNAL:-   "Barrage 'Q' Sector".
       SENT BY:-   Right Divisional Artillery or Right Group
                      Right Divisional Artillery to 60th
                      Divisional Artillery or Left Group
                      60th Divisional Artillery.
       ACTION BY:-   60th Divisional Artillery.

Battery.	Target.
One 4.5" Howitzer Battery.	Trench Junction S.22.c.27.8. S.22.a.1.0. S.21.b.95.1. S.22.a.1.6.
Two 18-pdr. Batteries.	Trench S.22.c.1.5. - S.22.c.4.65. S.22.a.2.05.- S.22.a.35.2.- S.22.a.1.6.

APPENDIX "E.3."

SUPPORT OF VI CORPS BY XVII CORPS.

(a) SITUATION.   Minor attack on VI Corps Left Flank.

SIGNAL.   "Barrage KAPPA".

SENT BY   Left Group 35th Division to Right Group 60th Division.

ACTION TAKEN BY   60th Divisional Artillery.

Group.	Battery.	Target.
Right.	1 18-pdr. Batty.	Enfilade C.T's. A.23.b.4.2. to A.23.d.1.8. and A.24.c.0.9. to A.23.d.70.35.
	1 18-pdr. Batty.	Barrage Trench A.23.b.1.3. to A.24.c.10.95.
Centre.	1 Section 4.5" Hows.	Barrage Trench Junctions A.24.a.15.90 and A.17.d.4.2.
	Remaining Batteries.	Stand by ready to reinforce Right Group Barrage if required.

(b) SITUATION.   Serious attack on VI Corps Left.

SIGNAL.   "Defend 35th Division Left.

SENT BY   35th Division to 60th Division.

ACTION TAKEN BY   60th Divisional Artillery.

Group.	Battery.	Co-ordinates of Battery positions.	Target.	Remarks.
Right.	4 18-pdr. Batteries.	G.10.c.20.05. G.10.c.70.60. G.10.c.20.85. G.2.c.75.10.	Barrage front trenches on flank of attack and reinforce 35th Division Barrage in Square A.23.	All immediately available.
Centre.	1 Section 4.5" Hows. 1 Section 4.5" Hows.	F.30.a.25.95. F.30.a.25.95.	Trench Junction A.24.b.3.9. Trench Junctions. A.24.b.6.5. & 7.4.	
Left.	1 18-pdr.Batty. 1 18-pdr.Batty.	F.18.c.20.25. A.7.d.80.25.	Enfilade Trench from A.24.b.3.9. to A.23.a.5.9.	Available if they can be spared,after having run guns out of emplacements to prepared sites in the open.
Centre.	1 18-pdr.Batty. 1 18-pdr.Batty. 1 18-pdr.Batty. 1 18-pdr.Batty.	F.30.a.30.76. F.30.a.45.54. F.24.c.50.50. A.26.a.25.65.	Pull out ready to reinforce 35th Divl. Arty. Fire on Squares A.30. G.6, or on A.29. and G.5, as the situation develops and as ordered by 35th Division.	

APPENDIX "E.4."

SUPPORT OF XVII CORPS BY VI CORPS.

(a) **SITUATION.**   Minor Attack on XVII Corps Right.
    SIGNAL.   "Barrage 'L' Sector.
    SENT BY   Right Group 60th Division to Left Group 35th Division.
    ACTION TAKEN BY.   35th Divisional Artillery.

Group.	Battery.	Target.
35th Bde.	1 18-pdr. Batty.	Enfilade Trenches A.22.b.6.5. to A.16.d.8.3. and A.22.b.80.45. to A.16.d.95.30.
	1 Section 4.5" Hows.	Shell Trench Junctions A.23.a.3.7. and A.24.a.0.3½.

(b) **SITUATION.**   Serious attack on XVII Corps Right.
    SIGNAL.   "Defend 60th Division Right."
    SENT BY   60th Division to 35th Division.
    ACTION TAKEN BY   35th Divisional Artillery.

Group.	Battery.	Target.
Left Bde.	2 or more 18-pdr. batteries (as available.)	Enfilade Trench from A.23.b.0.5. to A.11.d.6.5.
	1 Section 4.5" Hows.	Trench Junction A.17.d.3.2.
	1 Section 4.5" Hows.	Trench crossing LILLE ROAD at A.16.d.5½.1.
Centre & Left Bdes.	at least 2 of remaining 18-pdr. Batteries (as available).	Ready to bring enfilade fire to bear on an attack on ECURIE in squares A.22 and A.23. as the situation develops and as requested by 60th Division.

APPENDIX "E.5."

HEAVY ARTILLERY.

SUPPORT OF 60th DIVISION BY XVII CORPS HEAVY ARTILLERY.

Signal.   "S.O.S. LEFT".

Sent by   H.Q. 60th Division to H.Q. XVII Corps Heavy Artillery.

Action taken by XVII Corps Heavy Artillery.

Battery.	Target.
88th Siege Battery.	S.23.c.80.95.
	S.29.d.7.2.
220 m.m. Battery.	S.18.c.9.2.

Signal.   "S.O.S. CENTRE".

Sent by.   H.Q., 60th Division to H.Q., XVII Corps Heavy Artillery.

Action taken by XVII Corps Heavy Artillery.

Battery.	Target.
88th Siege Battery.	A.12.d.66.
	S.29.d.72.
220 m.m. Battery.	B.1.c.68.

Signal.   "S.O.S. RIGHT".

Sent by.   H.Q., 60th Division to H.Q., XVII Corps Heavy Artillery.

Action taken by XVII Corps Heavy Artillery.

Battery.	Target.
88th Siege Battery.	A.12.d.66.
	A.24.b.29.
220 m.m. Battery.	B.19.d.24.

Note:- (1) Rate of fire, one round per minute on each point in all cases.

(2) Remainder of Group will at once neutralize hostile batteries normally active in the area named. Fire will be opened at once on receipt of message "S.O.S. LEFT", "S.O.S. CENTRE" or "S.O.S. RIGHT", on the batteries which have been previously allotted by the Group Commander. This allotment will be constantly revised and kept up to date as positions and activity of hostile batteries alter. Opening rate of fire for counter batteries will be two rounds per section per minute.

APPENDIX "F".

CIRCULAR MEMORANDUM No. 4.

HOSTILE GAS ATTACK.

1. For the purpose of giving the alarm in case of a hostile Gas Attack, Gongs will be placed at the following points:-
   - 1 per Platoon in Front and Support Lines.
   - 1 at each Company, Battery, Battalion and Infantry and Artillery Headquarters, the Headquarters of each Field Company, Field Ambulance, Company Divisional Train, and Tunnelling Company in Brigade Reserve Lines.

   Strombos Horns will be placed in position and in charge of a sentry, as follows:-
   - 1 at each Battalion and Infantry Brigade Headquarters.
   - 1 at Town Majors' offices, Neuville St. Vaast and Maroeuil.
   - 1 at Headquarters, MAISON BLANCHE defence.
   - 1 at Headquarters, ECURIE defences.
   - 1 at each Headquarters, Artillery Group.

   The Gas Alarm once started is to be taken up at once by all sentries over Gongs and Horns.

2. In addition to above Signals, the following signal messages will be sent from all battalion Headquarters in line to affiliated Artillery Battery and Infantry Brigade Headquarters. The Infantry Brigade Headquarters will send these messages to the Brigades on their right and left, their Rear Brigade Headquarters, to Divisional Headquarters and all troops in their sector including their affiliated Artillery Group:-

   GAS RIGHT SECTOR.
   GAS CENTRE SECTOR.
   GAS LEFT SECTOR.
   GAS DIVISION ON RIGHT.
   GAS DIVISION ON LEFT.

   according to section on which the hostile gas attack is made. The Divisional Headquarters will inform the Corps, Heavy Artillery and neighbouring Divisions.

3. The necessary number of copies of the above messages should be kept ready for despatch in each signal office with a list of the units which the office is required to inform in case of hostile gas attack. C.R.A., C.R.E., and G.O.C's sectors and subordinate commanders will satisfy themselves from time to time that the necessary arrangements affecting the warning of their units are correct.

GAS ALERT.

1. Signal for Gas Alert, which will be "GALERT", will be given when the wind is favourable for a hostile gas attack. This signal should emanate from Divisional Headquarters but may be given by Brigades and even Battalions, should a sudden change of the wind take place, favourable to enemy.

   On receipt of this signal by night a sentry will be posted at each dug-out, whose duty it will be to wake all officers and men sleeping close by, in case of gas attack. All helmets will be worn in the "Alert" position, e.g., pinned on the shirt.

2. Cancel Gas Alert Signal, which will be "CANCEL GALERT", will be sent by Divisional Headquarters when wind becomes favourable to us.

PRACTICE GAS ALARMS.

Practice Gas Alarms will be carried out periodically under orders to be issued from Divisional Headquarters.
In such cases, sound signals will NOT be used but the passing of the alarm will be done by telephone.

P.T.O.

(2)

The time taken by units to stand to, ready to meet gas attack will be noted and reported by C.R.A., C.R.E., and G.O's.C. Brigades to Divisional Headquarters.

On receipt of the Practice/Gas Alarm Signal, which will be "PROVE GALERT":-

(i) All officers and other ranks east of the Chausee Brunehaut will at once put on gas helmet and goggles. Steps will be taken to ensure that everyone knows how to put these on, and has them properly adjusted.
(ii) All dug-outs will be closed by letting down the medicated blankets.
(iii) All troops will stand to outside dug-outs, except signallers on duty.
(iv) Troops in front and support lines will go to their alarm post, but no man other than the usual sentries, is to look over the parapet.
(v) Co. Gas N.C.Os. and men for Vermorel Sprayers will man them. These men must be checked to ensure that they know how to use the sprayers, etc.

This practice will be carried out by night as well as by day, so as to ensure that the system of rousing all officers and men in dug-outs is satisfactory.

The order to Dismiss will be given by G.O's.C. sectors to troops other than artillery when they are satisfied that all is correct.

The C.R.A. will give the order to dismiss to the Artillery.

H.Q., 60th Division.
1st August 1916.

E.T. Humphreys
Lieut-Colonel.
General Staff.

Note: It is unnecessary to replace Gas Helmets until they have been worn in the "Alert" position for a total period of 28 days.

APPENDIX "G".

ARRANGEMENTS FOR EVACUATING CASUALTIES FROM FRONT AREA.

(1) 2/4 Lond. Amb. collects and evacuates casualties from the Left and Centre Sectors. 2/6 Lond. Amb. from the Right Sector.

(2) Left and Centre Sectors.

    (a). Collecting Posts are at :-
        (i). A.8.b.6.8. Neuville St. Vaast.
        (ii). A.9.c.1.5. Post Centrale.
    (b) Advanced Dressing Station for this area is at A.8.c.5.5. Aux Rietz.
    (c) Evacuation from Aux Rietz to Main Dressing Station is by Ambulance Car at night; by Territorial Avenue by day. In case of extreme urgency and if conditions permit, Car may go to Aux Rietz by day.

(3) Right Sector.

    (a) Collecting Posts are at :-
        (i). A.28.c.1.1. Route de Lille.
        (ii). A.26.d.9.4. Madagascar.
        (iii). A.20.d.5.7. near Ariane.
    (b) Advanced Dressing Station for this Area is at G.7.b.8.8. Anzin ST. Aubin.

(4) The Divisional Rest Station formed by 2/5 Lond. Amb. is at Haute Avesnes.

(5) Medical Officers in charge of Units, on taking over an Aid Post, should immediately report their arrival and exact position of Aid Post, by Map reference if possible, to the Officer in Charge, Advanced Dressing Station.

(6) Units which are not actually in the Trenches, yet stationed in the Front Area (such as Batteries) will likewise communicate with Advanced Dressing Stations to secure the removal of casualties.

(7) These arrangements apply to the collection of Sick as well as wounded.

(8) A Medical Inspection Room has been established in Maroeuil for the details billetted in Maroeuil who have no Medical Officers. A Medical Officer will be there daily from 9 a.m. to 10 a.m.

H.Q., 60th Division.
11/7/16.

SECRET.

Vol 5

WAR DIARY.

GENERAL STAFF, 60th (LONDON) DIVISION.

FROM - 1st OCTOBER 1916.

TO - 31st OCTOBER 1916.

Army Form C. 2118

WAR DIARY
or
INTELLIGENCE SUMMARY
(Erase heading not required.)

Instructions regarding War Diaries and Intelligence Summaries are contained in F.S. Regs., Part II. and the Staff Manual respectively. Title Pages will be prepared in manuscript.

Place	Date	Hour	Summary of Events and Information	Remarks and references to Appendices
HERMAVILLE	1st	4.36am	Division report situation normal. Muster patrols sent out.	Ops
"	"	6.10am	Division report enemy blew camouflet at 4.45 am near S.28.a.28.89. No casualties and no damage to our trenches. Underground situation not yet known.	Ops
"	"	8.10am	Division report enemy blew two camouflets simultaneously, one no already reported and other at S.28.a.48.50. Right gallery of our mine undamaged but gassed. No casualties. Under ground situation of first camouflet still unknown.	G.2
"	"	4.30pm	Division report situation quiet except in left sector where hostile M.Guns T.M. too again been found opposite left 1. and doing damage. Weather fine. Wind E.SE.	Ops Ops
"	2nd	2.40am	Division report enemy trenches at S.28.a.5.4. entered by raiding party at 2 am. No Germans were seen and trench was badly damaged. A dug-out was found empty. All party returned. Casualties 6 wounded. At about 2 a.m. enemy T.M. fired a few rounds in retaliation.	Ops Ops
"	"	4.20am	Division report except for raid situation normal. Wind N.E.	Ops
"	"	4.20pm	Division report quiet day. Wind S.	Ops
"	"	"	Weather wet. Rain continuous all day. Wind S.E. 15 S.	Ops
"	3rd	4.33am	Division report situation normal. Wind N.E.	Ships 10
"	"	4.40pm	Division report situation normal. Wind S.W.	Ops
"	"	10.7pm	Division report we blew camouflet near DEVON crater at S.28 a 4.0 at 7 pm. No crater formed. Gap leading to DEVON damaged. Weather wet in morning, fine in afternoon. Wind S.W.	Ops
"	4th	4.33am	Division report situation normal. Wind N.E.	Ops
"	"	4.22pm	Division report situation normal. Nothing to report. Wind S.W.	Ops

Army Form C. 2118

WAR DIARY
or
INTELLIGENCE SUMMARY
(Erase heading not required.)

Instructions regarding War Diaries and Intelligence Summaries are contained in F.S. Regs, Part II. and the Staff Manual respectively. Title Pages will be prepared in manuscript.

Place	Date	Hour	Summary of Events and Information	Remarks and references to Appendices
HERMAVILLE	4th	10.55pm	Division report 1 officer and 5 men 2/20th London Regt. raided enemy trenches at 7.15pm near S.22.22.23. Four Germans killed and others wounded. Our casualties one killed and two 2/4 4th wounded. All gas casualties brought back. No identifications obtained owing to enemy wire. Weather wet.	See A/3
"	5th	4.45pm	Division report situation unchanged. Wind S.W.	See A/4 See A/5 See A/6 See A/7
"	"	11.35pm	Division report situation normal. No unusual activity to report. Wind S.W. Weather fair.	See A/8
"	6th	6.30am	Division report situation unchanged. Wind S.W.	See A/9
"	"	12.40pm	Division report enemy blew camouflet at 9.57am near S.28.c.48.90. Surface broken & fissure formed about 30 yards long. Our S. gallery probably destroyed & support line considerably damaged. No casualties.	See A/10
"	"	4.40pm	Division report situation normal. Wind S.W. Weather fair. Strong wind.	See A/11
"	7th	4.20am	Division report situation normal. Nothing to report.	See A/12
"	"	4.35pm	Division report situation normal. Wind S.W. Weather cold in afternoon. Wind S.W. strong.	See A/13
"	8th	4.38am	Division report situation unchanged. Wind Westerly. Sixteen patrols were out.	See A/14
"	"	4.42pm	Division report situation unchanged. Wind S.W.	See A/15
"	"	7.26pm	Division report 2/22nd London Regt raided enemy trenches about A.16.a.6.4. at 6.57pm. Three unwounded and one wounded prisoners belonging to 107th Reserve Regiment captured.	See A/16

WAR DIARY
or
INTELLIGENCE SUMMARY
(Erase heading not required.)

Army Form C. 2118

Place	Date	Hour	Summary of Events and Information	Remarks and references to Appendices
HERMAVILLE	9th	2.35 AM	Division report 2/17th London Regt raided enemy trenches at S.28.A.6.4. Six prisoners belonging to 104th Reserve Regiment taken. Whole party have returned and no casualties reported at present. Time of starting 1.50 AM. No immediate retaliation but hostile TMs now active on the western parts of the left sector.	See 185
"	"	4.35 AM	Division report situation normal.	See 185
"	"	4.35 PM	Division report situation normal. Some hostile TM activity in centre sector except for the two raids previously mentioned.	See 185
"	"	10 PM	Division report raid by 2/18th London Regt at S.22.c.2.5 at 8 p.m. completed. Encountered rifle fire and bombs. No prisoners.	See 185
"	10th	12.45 AM	Division reports our casualties in raid 10.r. killed. 3 off + 28 o.r. wounded and 6 missing, but numbers not yet certain. Enemy trenches strongly manned. Holding parties got into enemy trenches and claim to have bayonetted many Germans.	Cas
"	"	4.30 AM	Division report situation quiet.	Cas
"	"	4.45 PM	Division report situation normal. Enemy aeroplane brought down at 3.15 p.m. by Lewis Gunners in left sector. Drs fell in enemy lines opposite P.73.	Cas
"	"		Weather fine. Wind S.W.	
"	11th	4.40 AM	Division report situation normal. Enemy Trench Mortars Centre II very Count Xabe Ry casualties. Enemy trench mortars have damaged our front trenches.	Cas
"	"	7.45 AM	Division report enemy raided PULPIT Crater early this morning. We are drawn off, leaving b.733 R.r. Regt one killed) one wounded (E) + one unwounded prisoner all belonging to 164th R.r. Regt.	Cas
"	"	4.35 PM	Division report enemy attempted to raid our trenches about A.4.d.3.2 at 5 am this morning. They were repulsed, enemy losing 6 killed one wounded 3 our unwounded prisoner (property clothes he suffered). Further casualties as rifles as rifles were caught by L.G. fire later. Enemy suffering difficulties otherwise normal. Weather fine but dull. Wind strong S.W.	Cas Cas

Army Form C. 2118

WAR DIARY
or
INTELLIGENCE SUMMARY
(Erase heading not required.)

Instructions regarding War Diaries and Intelligence Summaries are contained in F.S. Regs., Part II and the Staff Manual respectively. Title Pages will be prepared in manuscript.

Place	Date	Hour	Summary of Events and Information	Remarks and references to Appendices
HERMAVILLE	12th	4.40am	Division report situation normal. Wind W.S.W. Intermittent T.M. fire on right.	CRA
"	"	4.30pm	Division report situation unchanged. Wind strong. S.S.W.	CRA
"	"		Weather dull. Strong wind S.S.W.	CRA
"	13th	4.35am	Division report situation normal.	CRA
"	"	4.50pm	Division report situation normal except for some hostile T.M. activity on Centre 2.	CRA
"	"		Weather dull. Wind S.W.	CRA
"	14th	1.20am	Division report that about 20 of enemy attempted to cross LILLE ROAD and BIDOT trench about 10.10pm but were driven off by rifle fire.	CRA
"	"	4.25am	Division report situation normal.	CRA
"	"	4.40pm	Division report situation normal.	CRA
"	15th	3.55am	Division report 2/23rd Lond. R. raided enemy trench as notified. Nearly all raiders have returned but no information yet received as to prisoners being taken.	CRA
"	"	4.30am	Division report further details about raid on A.23.d.9.8. Two dugouts in which it is known there were Germans were bombed. Two men reported missing. Situation otherwise normal. Of the missing one was known to be killed and the other mortally wounded.	CRA
"	"	4.40pm	Division report situation normal. Weather dull but fine at intervals. Wind S.W. strong.	CRA
"	16th	4.25am	Division have nothing unusual to report.	CRA
"	"	4.30pm	Division report our artillery, heavy machine guns & light T.M's continued with Corps Heavy Artillery in bombardment of enemy T.M. emplacements and trenches from 8.30am till 11.45am and from 1.30pm onwards. Results appear very satisfactory and bombardment still continuing. Enemy retaliated very feebly with T.M. only. Situation otherwise normal. Weather fine variable got less N.W.	CRA
"	17th	4.35am	Division report situation normal.	CRA
"	"	4.40pm	Division report considerable hostile T.M. and artillery activity on our front line in Centre 1. Situation otherwise normal. Weather fine. Wind N.W.	CRA

1875 Wt. W593/826 1,000,000 4/15 J.B.C. & A. A.D.S.S./Forms/C. 2118.

Army Form C. 2118

WAR DIARY
or
INTELLIGENCE SUMMARY
(Erase heading not required.)

Instructions regarding War Diaries and Intelligence Summaries are contained in F.S. Regs, Part II. and the Staff Manual respectively. Title Pages will be prepared in manuscript.

Place	Date	Hour	Summary of Events and Information	Remarks and references to Appendices
HERMAVILLE	18th	4.20am	Division report situation normal	Cmd
"	18th	4.45pm	Division report hostile T.M. very active on centre sector to which our Artillery have replied with effect	Cmd
"	"	"	Situation otherwise normal. Wind N.W.	Cmd
"	19th	4.20am	Weather fair but dull with some showers	Cmd
"	"	"	Division report situation normal.	Cmd
"	"	4.45pm	Division report situation normal.	Cmd
"	19th	4.25pm	Operation Order No 2 issued as to relief of Division by 3rd Canadian Division	App. B
"	"	"	Weather cont. Wind N.W.	Cmd
"	20	4.30am	Division report situation normal.	Cmd
"	"	10.15am	Division report enemy aeroplane compelled to make forced descent by our Lewis Guns approximate about S. 29 a. S.3.	Cmd
"	"	4.45pm	Division report enemy T.Ms active on left 2 subsector. otherwise normal.	Cmd
"	"	"	Weather fine & cold. Wind N.E.	Cmd
"	21	4.30am	Division report situation normal. Wind N.E.	Cmd
"	"	4.40pm	Division report hostile T.Ms active on Centre 2 all morning otherwise normal wind N E	Cmd
"	"	"	Weather fine cold. Wind N.E.	Cmd
"	22	4.40am	Division report situation normal. Wind S.E. to S.S.W.	Cmd
"	"	4.35pm	Division report Minnows normal. Hostile T.M. active on left of Centre sector between 7 and 8 am. and 1.30 to 3pm. Wind S.E.	Cmd
"	"	"	Weather misty but fair. Wind S.E.	Cmd
"	23.	4.35am	Division report situation normal.	Cmd
"	"	4.38pm	Division report situation normal. Hostile T.M. active at intervals on Centre 2.	Cmd
"	"	"	Operation Order No 3 +4 issued. Weather wet and misty. Wind S.E.	Cmd

Army Form C. 2118

WAR DIARY
or
INTELLIGENCE SUMMARY
(Erase heading not required.)

Instructions regarding War Diaries and Intelligence Summaries are contained in F. S. Regs., Part II. and the Staff Manual respectively. Title Pages will be prepared in manuscript.

Place	Date	Hour	Summary of Events and Information	Remarks and references to Appendices
HERMAVILLE	25.	4 p.m.	Division report situation normal.	Ind
"	"	4.45 p.m.	Division report situation normal.	Ind
"	"		Weather dull with some showers, wind S.E.	Ind
HOUVIN	26.	4.40 p.m.	Operation Orders No 3 & 4 issued. Division report situation normal.	Ind App C.
HOUVIGNEUL	"	10 a.m.	Divisional HQ left HERMAVILLE and established HOUIN HOUVIGNEUL and First & 3rd Armies informed.	Ind
"	"		Weather wet, misty, wind S.E. (see Artillery)	Ind
"	27.	1.45 p.m.	Division First Army wires that 30 Div will be transferred temporarily to Reserve Army and will not be attached to fourth Army.	Ind
"	"		Weather fair with showers. Wind S.E.	Ind
FROHEN LE GRAND	28.	10 a.m.	Div. HQ established at FROHEN LE GRAND. Division continues move southward (see Artillery)	Ind
"	"		Operation Orders No 5 & 6 issued.	Ind
BERNAVILLE	29.	10 a.m.	Div. HQ established at BERNAVILLE. Division continues move southward. (see Artillery)	Ind
"	"		Weather wet. Strong S.W. wind.	Ind
"	29	12.5 a.m.	Division ordered to send 2 Fd Co to FAMECHON and they went accordingly.	Ind
"	"		Division ordered to send 1 Fd Co to Res. Army HQ at TOUTENCOURT as soon as possible.	Ind
"	30	9 a.m.	2/4 Fd Co. left for TOUTENCOURT at 9 a.m. Weather wet. Strong wind S.W.	Ind
"	31.	9.30 a.m.	G.S.O.1 visited Adv. G.H.Q. and received instructions re move of Div. to new area and return of Field Coys & Div. Arty.	Ind
"	"	7.20 p.m.	Orders received from 15 Corps for the Div. to move to No 6 Area by Noon 3rd & 4th.	Ind
"	"		Weather showery. Wind W. strong	Ind

1875 Wt. W593/826 1,000,000 4/15 J.B.C. & A. A.D.S.S./Forms/C. 2118.

Army Form C. 2118

WAR DIARY
or
~~INTELLIGENCE SUMMARY~~
(Erase heading not required.)

Instructions regarding War Diaries and Intelligence Summaries are contained in F.S. Regs., Part II. and the Staff Manual respectively. Title Pages will be prepared in manuscript.

Place	Date	Hour	Summary of Events and Information	Remarks and references to Appendices
	Oct. 30. 1916.		A. Wilson Golam Col. bo Division	

War Diary

Copy No. 24

SECRET.

60th DIVISION ORDER No. 2.

19th October 1916.

1. The 60th Division (less Artillery) will be relieved by the 3rd Canadian Division (less Artillery) during the period 23/26th October.

    The 60th Division is to be concentrated in the new Area, as shown in Table "D" by midnight, 27/28th October. Bde Area Commanders are responsible for the allotment of billets in their Area.

2. The relief of the Inf. Bdes. and their marches to the new Area will be carried out in accordance with Tables "A", "B" and "C".

    All arrangements as to guides and times of reliefs will be made between Bde. Commanders concerned.

    Bde. Commanders will hand over command of their Sectors on completion of relief.

    Completion of relief of each Unit to be reported to this Office and repeated to the 3rd Canadian Division.

3. The 3" T.M.Battys. and Bde. M.G. Cos. will be relieved under arrangements to be made between Bde. Commanders concerned, who will also issue the orders for their march to the new Area.

    The M.G.Co., when proceeding to the new Area, is to march with one of the Inf. Bns. of the Bde. to which it belongs.

4. The Field Cos. R.E., and 1/12 L.N.Lancs. R., will be relieved under arrangements between the O's. R.E.

    The C.R.E. will issue orders for the march of the Field Cos. to the new Area.

    The detachment, 1/12 L.N.Lancs. R., now working on the railway will be relieved by the Pioneer Bn., 3rd Canadian Division, between 4 p.m., 23rd Oct, and 6 p.m., 26th Oct.

    The 1/12 L.N.Lancs. R. will move to FERME DOFFINE on the 25th Oct. Route:- ETRUN - HERMAVILLE. It will move to LIENCOURT on the 26th. Times of starting and route to LIENCOURT to be settled by the C.C.

5. The relief of the Administrative Units and their marches to the new Area will be arranged by the A.A. & Q.M.G.

6. The following personnel is to remain with the Unit relieved, and will rejoin their (present) Rear Bde. H.Q. at 10 a.m., 27th inst., whence they will proceed in lorries to rejoin their Units.

    3 linesmen with each Bde. Sec. Signal Co.
    1 Officer and 8 N.C.O's with each Bn. (except that in Div.Res.)
    1 Officer and 2 N.C.O's with each 3" T.M.Batty.
    1 Officer per Co. and 1 man (per gun in the line relieved) with each Bde. M.G. Co.

    The above will be rationed and quartered by the Unit to which they are attached.

7. All Trench Maps and photos. are to be handed over to relieving units.

8. A list of Trench Stores handed over, is to be given to incoming units. Instructions on this subject are being issued.

9. Refilling points will be detailed later.

10. Command of the front remains in the hands of the G.O.C., 60th Div. until 10 a.m. 26th instant, at which hour Div. H.Q. will open at LE CAUROY.

- 2 -

11. A copy of the orders issued for the reliefs and move to the New Area is to be forwarded to this office.

12. Acknowledge.

E. T. Humphreys
Lieut-Colonel.
General Staff.

Copies issued at 7.45 pm.

To. A.D.C. (for G.O.C.)
179 Inf. Bde.
180 Inf. Bde.
181 Inf. Bde.
C.R.A.
C.R.E.
"A".
A.D.M.S.
Signals.
1/12 L.N.Lancs. R.

Div. Train.
Div. Supply Column.
A.D.V.S.
Camp Commandant.
XVII Corps.
3rd Canadian Division.
24th Division.
35th Division.
Controller of Mines.
War Diary.
File.

TABLE "A".   RELIEF OF 179 INFANTRY BRIGADE BY 9th CANADIAN INFANTRY BRIGADE.

179 Inf. Bde.   9th Can. Inf. Bde.

Date.	Bde.H.Q.	2/13.Bn.	2/14 Bn.	2/15 Bn.	2/16 Bn.	W.Bn.	X. Bn.	Y. Bn.	Z. Bn.	Remarks.
22nd.	A.8.d.2.5.	C.2.	C.1.	BRAY.	Bde.Res.	'	'	'	'	
23rd.	do.	C.2.	C.1.	TILLOY & HERMAVILLE	Bde.Res.	MAROEU- IL.	BRAY.	'	'	
24th.	do.	BOIS DES ALLEUX, MONT ST. ELOY, ECOIVRES.	C.1.	New Area.	BRAY.	Bde.Res.	C.2.	MAROEU- IL.	'	VASE Trench allotted to 181 Inf.Bde. for their relief.
25th	ECOIVRES.	do.	MAROEU- IL.	do.	TILLOY & HERMA- VILLE.	do.	do.	C.1.	'	
26th	HOUVIN.	New Area.	TILLOY & HERMA- VILLE.	do.	New Area.	'	'	'	BRAY.	
27th	do.	do.	New Area.	do.	do.	'	'	'	'	

New Area is:- HOUVIN -HOUVIGNEUL -MAGNICOURT-sur-Canche -HONVAL -SIBIVILLE -SERICOURT -SARS--les--Bois -Petit BOURET-sur-Cancho.

Routes to New Area are:- HAUTE AVESNES -HERMAVILLE -TILLOY--LES--HERMAVILLE -IZEL--LES--HAMEAU -VILLERS--SIRE SIMON - AMBRINES.

TABLE "B".   RELIEF OF 180 INFANTRY BRIGADE BY 7th CANADIAN INFANTRY BRIGADE.

	180 Inf. Bde.					7th Canadian Infantry Brigade.			
Date. Oct.	Bde.H.Q.	2/17th Battn.	2/18th Battn.	2/19th Battn.	2/20th Battn.	W.Battn.	X.Battn.	Y.Battn.	Z.Battn. Remarks.
22nd	A.8.c.7.9.	L.1.	L.2.	Bde.Res.	BOIS des ALLEUX.	"	"	"	"
23rd	-do-	L.1.	L.2.	Bde.Res.	PENIN.	BOIS des ALLEUX	EGOIVRES.	"	"
23/24th	-do-	L.1.	L.2.	BOIS des ALLEUX.	-do-	Bde.Res.	NEUVILLE ST.VAAST.	"	"
24th	-do-	Bde. Res. NEUVILLE ST.VAAST.	-do-	-do-	New Area.	L.1.	L.2.	EGOIVRES.	"
24/25th	MONT ST. ELOY.	EGOI- VRES.	ACQ.	-do-	-do-	-do-	-do-	Bde. Res.	"
25th	BUNE- VILLE.	-do-	-do-	PENIN.	-do-	-do-	-do-	-do-	BOIS des ALLEUX.
26th	-do-	PENIN.	-do-	New Area.	-do-				
27th	-do-	New Area.	New Area.	-do-	-do-				

New Area is :- BUNEVILLE - MONCHEAUX - MONTS-en-TERNOIS - GOUY-en-TERNOIS - MAIZIERES - PETIT HOUVIN.

Routes to New Area are :- ACQ - road junction on ARRAS-ST.POL Road ân HAUTE AVESNES - SAVY- BERLES - PENIN.

Table 3.   RELIEF OF 181st INFANTRY BRIGADE BY 8th CANADIAN INFANTRY BRIGADE.

181st Infantry Brigade.   8th Canadian Infantry Brigade.

Date.	Bde.H.Q.	2/21 Bn.	2/22 Bn.	2/23 Bn.	2/24 Bn.	W.Bn.	X.Bn.	Y.Bn.	Z.Bn.	Remarks.
22	ETRUN.	R.1.	R.2.	ETRUN	Bde.Res.	-	-	-	-	
23	do	do	do	IZEL LES HAMEAU	do	MAROEUIL	ETRUN	-	-	
24	do	do	ETRUN	MAROEUIL & then to IZEL LES HAMEAU.	MAROEUIL Bde.Res.	R.2.	MAROEUIL	-	Vase C.T. allotted to 181 Inf.Bde. for this relief.
25	EBREUVE	MAROEUIL	IZEL LES HAMEAU	do	New Area	do	do	R.1.	ETRUN.	
26	do	IZEL LES HAMEAU.	New Area	do	do	-	-	-	-	
27	do	New Area	do	do	do	-	-	-	-	

New area is :- REBREUVE - RUBREUVIETTE - BERLENCOURT - DENIER - CANETTEMONT - BTREE WAMIN

Routes to New area are :- HABARCQ - Cross roads S. of IZEL les HAMEAU - MANIN - GIVENCHY le NOBLE - LIGNEREUIL.

TABLE "D".

LE CAUROY. ....Div. H.Q.

180 Inf. Bde. Area.

    BUNEVILLE   Bde. H.Q.)   Troops.
    MONCHEAUX.
    MONTS-en-TERNOIS.   180 Inf. Bde.
    GOUY-en-TERNOIS.   1/6 Fd. Co. R.E.
    MAIZIERES.   2/5 Field Amb.
    PETIT HOUVIN.

179 Inf. Bde. Area.

    HOUVIN.   Bde. H.Q.)
    HOUVIGNEUL.   Troops.
    MAGNICOURT sur Canche.
    HONVAL.   179 Inf. Bde.
    SIBIVILLE.   2/4 Field Co. R.E.
    SERICOURT.   2/4 Field Amb.
    SARS les Bois.
    PETIT BOURET sur Canche.)

181 Inf. Bde. Area.

    REBREUVE.   Bde. H.Q.)
    REBREUVIETTE.   Troops.
    BERLENCOURT.
    DENIER.   181 Inf. Bde.
    CANETTEMONT.   3/3 Field Co. R.E.
    ETREE - WAMIN.   2/6 Field Amb.

    LIENCOURT.   1/12 L.N.Lancs. R.

    GRAND BOURET.   (60 Div. Supply Column.
                                 (60 Mob. Vet. Sec.

    WAMIN.   60 Div. Train.

    LE CAUROY.   60 San. Sec.

War Diary

SECRET.   G.S./393/11.

H.Q., 179th Inf. Bde.   H.Q., 1/12 L.N.Lancs. R.
  "   180th   "   "   "   Div. Train.
  "   181st   "   "   "   Div. Supply Column.
C.R.A.   A.D.V.S.
C.R.E.   Camp Commandant.
A.D.M.S.   XVII Corps.
60 Div. Signals.   "A".

Reference Map, LENS Sheet 11.

      The following amendments and additions to 60 Div. Op.Order No.2, Tables "A", "B", and "C" are to be made :-

      Routes for Inf. Bdes. will be changed as under :-

179 Inf. Bde.   Same as already issued and on via MAGNICOURT and HOUVIN.

180 Inf. Bde.   Same as already issued and on via MAIZIERES.

181 Inf. Bde.   HABARCQ - IZEL les Hameau - PENIN or GIVENCHY le Noble.

C.A.Bolton. Captain
G.S.
for Lieut-Colonel,
General Staff.

22nd Oct. 1916.
    Issued at 7.0 p.m.

War Diary.

SECRET.   G.S./392/14.

H.Q.179th.Inf.Bde.	H.Q. 1/12th.L.N.Lancs.R.
180th. ,, ,,	Div. Train.
181st. ,, ,,	Div. Supply Column.
C.R.A.	A.D.V.S.
C.R.E.	Camp Commandant.
A.D.M.S.	XVII Corps.
60th.Div.Signals.	"A".

Ref.Map. LENS Sheet. 11.

(1) Table D issued from this office on the 21st.Oct. giving the allotment of areas in the New Area is cancelled and the following substituted:-

HOUVIN HOUVIGNEUL.   Div. H. Q.

179th.Inf.Bde.Area.   Troops.
SERICOURT ..... Bde.H.Q.
SIBIVILLE.
BUNEVILLE.   179th.Inf.Bde.
MONTS EN TERNOIS.   2/4th.Fd.Co.R.E.
MONCHEAUX.   2/4th.Fd.Amb.
HONVAL.   Det. Train.
Routes HAUTE AVESNES - TILLOY - AMBRINES.

180th.Inf.Bde. Area.   Troops.
HOUVIN HOUVIGNEUL...Bde.H.Q.
HOUVIGNEUL.   180th.Inf.Bde.
CANETTEMONT.   1/6th.Fd.Co.R.E.
MAGNICOURT.   2/5th.Fd.Amb.
                                             Det.Train.
REBREUVE and PETIT BOURET are added to this area on the 26th.
Route ACQ - Road junction on ARRAS - St.POL road at HAUTE AVESNES - BERLES - PENIN.

181st. Inf. Bde. Area.   Troops.
BEAUDRICOURT. ... Bde. H.Q.
IVERGNY.   181st. Inf. Bde.
                                            3/3rd. Fd.Co. R.E.
                                            2/6th.Fd.Amb.
                                            Det. Train.
REBREUVIETTE - ROZIERE - WAMIN - ETREE WAMIN and OPPY will be added to this area on the 26th.
Route HERMAVILLE - IZEL LES HAMEAU - MANIN - LIENCOURT.

GOUY EN TERNOIS	1/12 L.N.Lancs R.
HOUVIN HOUVIGNEUL.	60th.Div.Supply Column.
	Det.Train.
	60th.San. Sec.
BROUILLY.	60th.Mob.Vet.Sec.

(2) Acknowledge.

23rd.October,1916.
Issued at Oppin.

                                                           Lieut.Col.
                                                           General Staff.

SECRET. 60th DIVISION ORDER NO. 3.   Copy No. 17
                                    25th October 1916.

Reference Map. LENS Sheet 11 1/100,000.

1. The 60th Division (less Artillery) moves South on the 28th October as under.
   It is to be clear of the DOULLENS - FREVENT - ST. POL Road by 12 noon.

Group.	Troops.	Starting Point.	Time.
A.	Div. H.Q.	Cross roads just W. of	8.0 a.m.
	60 San. Sec.	HOUVIN-HOUVIGNEUL.	8.10 a.m.
	Det. Train.	On road to FREVENT.	8.10 a.m.

Route. FREVENT - BONNIERES.

B.	179 Inf. Bde.	Road junction by S of	10.0 a.m.
	2/4 Fd. Co., R.E.	St. HILAIRE.	10.40 a.m.
	2/4 Fd. Amb.		10.45 a.m.
	Det. Train.		10.50 a.m.

Route. FREVENT - VACQUERIE le BOUCQ.

C.	180 Inf. Bde.	Cross roads by T in	10.0 a.m.
	1/6 Fd. Co., R.E.	GRAND BOURET.	10.40 a.m.
	2/5 Fd. Amb.		10.45 a.m.
	Det. Train.		10.50 a.m.

Route. Road junction on FREVENT - BOUQUEMAISON road
       about 1 mile S.W. of F in FREVENT - BONNIERES.

D.	181 Inf. Bde.	Cross roads at Southern	9.30 a.m.
	2/3 Fd. Co., R.E.	end of IVERGNY.	10.10 a.m.
	2/6 Fd. Amb.		10.15 a.m.
	Det. Train.		10.20 a.m.

Route. LE SOUICH - BOUQUEMAISON.

E.	1/12 L.H.	Road junction by G of	8.0 a.m.
	Lancs. R.	GOUY on TERNOIS.	

Route. ETREE WAMIN - REBREUVIETTE.

2. The 60 Mob. Vet. Sec. will move via REBREUVIETTE - ARBRE - BONNIERES starting at 8 a.m.

3. Div. H.Q. will close at HOUVIN - HOUVIGNEUL at 10 a.m. and re-open at FROHEN LE GRAND at same hour.

4. Acknowledge.

Issued at ......

Lieut-Colonel,
General Staff,

Copies to:-

A.D.C. (for G.O.C.)
179 Inf. Bde.
180 Inf. Bde.
181 Inf. Bde.
C.R.A.
C.R.E.
"A".
A.D.M.S.
Signals.
1/12 L.H.Lancs.R.

Div. Train.
Div. Supply Column.
A.D.V.S.
Camp Commandant.
3rd Army.
War Diary.
File.

SECRET.   Copy No. 17

                    60th DIVISION ORDER NO.4.
                    ─────────────────────────
                                                              25th October 1916.

1.   The 60th Division (less Artillery) will halt for the
        night 28/29 October in areas as under :-

        Designation
        of Area.   Troops.   Area.

        Div. H.Q.   Div. H.Q.   (FROHEN LE GRAND
        Area.   60 San. Sec.   (FROHEN LE PETIT.
                        Det. Train.
                        60 Mob. Vet. Sec.

        179 Bde.   179 Inf. Bde.   VILLERS L'HOPITAL - FORTEL -
        Area.   2/4 Fd. Co. R.E.   BOFFLES - NOEUX - WAVANS -
                        2/4 Fd. Amb.
                        Det. Train.   BEAUVOIR WAVANS - BEAUVOIR
                                            RIVIERE - BEALCOURT - St. ACHEUL.
                Bde. H.Q.   WAVANS.

        180 Bde.   180 Inf. Bde.   BONNIERES - REMAISNIL -
        Area.   1/6 Fd. Co. R.E.   MEZEROLLES - OUTREBOIS.
                        2/5 Fd. Amb.
                        Det. Train.

                Bde. H.Q.   REMAISNIL.

        181 Bde.   181 Inf. Bde.   NEUVILLETTE - BARLY - OCCOCHES -
        Area.   3/3 Fd. Co. R.E.   RANSART.
                        2/6 Fd. Amb.
                        Det. Train.

                Bde. H.Q.   OCCOCHES.

        Pioneer Bn.   1/12 L.N.Lancs.R.   CANTELEUX and BEAUVOIR
        Area.
                H.Q.   CANTELEUX.

2.   Refilling Point. On DOULLENS - AUXI LE CHATEAU road between
                          FROHEN LE GRAND and road junction about
                          2 miles W. of that place.
        Time will be notified later.

3.   Div. H.Q. will be at FROHEN-LE-GRAND.

4.   Acknowledge.

                                                    Lieut-Colonel.
                                                    General Staff.

Issued at..........

Copies to:-

        A.D.C. (for G.O.C.)   1/12 L.N.Lancs.R.
        179 Inf. Bde.   Div. Train.
        180 Inf. Bde.   Div. Supply Column.
        181 Inf. Bde.   A.D.V.S.
        C.R.A.   Camp Commandant.
        C.R.E.   3rd Army.
        "A"   War Diary.
        A.D.M.S.   File.
        Signals.

War Diary

SECRET.   Copy No. 19
                60th DIVISION ORDER No. 5.   28th October 1916.

Reference Map :- LENS, Sheet 11. 1/100000.

1. The 60th Division (less Artillery) continues its move
    South on the 29th October as under:-

    Group. Troops.   Starting Point.   Time.
    A.   Div. H.Q.   )   FROHEN LE PETIT   9. 0.a.m.
            60 San. Sec.   )   Cross roads.   9.10.a.m.
            60 Mob. Vet. Sec.)   9.10.a.m.

            Route :- LE MEILLARD.

    B.   179 Inf. Bde.   )   Road junction in   9.30.a.m.
            2/4 Fd.Co. R.E.   )   ST. ACHEUL.   10.20.a.m.
            2/4 Fd.Amb.   )   10.25.a.m.

            Route :- MONTIGNY LES JONGLEURS - PROUVILLE.

    C.   180 Inf. Bde.   )   Road junction   10. 0 a.m.
            1/6 Fd.Co. R.E.   )   Northern end of   10.40.a.m.
            2/5 Fd. Amb.   )   LE MEILLARD.   10.45.a.m.

            Route :- LE MEILLARD

    D.   181 Inf. Bde.   )   Road junction   9. 0 a.m.
            3/3 Fd.Co. R.E.   )   Southern end of   9.40.a.m.
            2/6 Fd. Amb.   )   OUTREBOIS.   9.45.a.m.

            Route :- AUTHIEUX - FIENVILLERS.

    E.   1/12 L.N.Lancs. R.   JANTELEUX cross-roads. 9.30 a.m.

            Route :- BARLY - - - - - OUTREBOIS.

2. Baggage Wagons will accompany their units.

3. Div. H.Q. will close at FROHEN LE GRAND at 10.0 a.m. and
    reopen at BERNAVILLE at same hour.

4. Acknowledge.
                                                C.H.Bolton. Captain.
Issued at... 12 noon
                                                    Lieut-Colonel.
Copies to:-   General Staff.

    A.D.C. (for G.O.C.)   1/12 L.N. Lancs. R.
    179 Inf. Bde.   Div. Train.
    180 Inf. Bde.   Div. Supply Column.
    181 Inf. Bde.   A.D.V.S.
    C.R.A.   Camp Commandant.
    C.R.E.   3rd Army.
    "A"   IV Corps.
    A.D.M.S.   War Diary.
    Signals.   File.

SECRET.　　　　　　　　　　　　　　　　　　　　　Copy No. **19**
　　60th DIVISION ORDER No. 6.
　　　　　　　　　　　　　　　　　　　　　　　28th October 1916.

Reference Map　LENS, Sheet 11, 1/100,000

1.　The 60th Division (less Artillery) will halt for the night 29/30th October as under:-

Designation of
Area.　　　　　　　　Troops.　　　　　　　　　Area.

Div. H.Q.　　　　　　Div. H.Q.　　　　)BERNAVILLE.
Area.　　　　　　　　60 San. Sec.　　　)
　　　　　　　　　　　Det. Train.　　　　)
　　　　　　　　　　　60 Mob. Vet. Sec.)

179 Bde.　　　　　　 179 Inf. Bde.　　　) MONTIGNY LES JONGLEURS
Area.　　　　　　　　2/4 Fd. Co.R.E.) GRIMONT-PROUVILLE-
　　　　　　　　　　　2/4 Fd. Amb.　　　) RIBEAUCOURT-BARLETTE-GENCOURT
　　　　　　　　　　　Det. Train.　　　　) St. HILAIRE-LANCHES-EPECAMPS
　　　　　　　　　　　　　　　　　　　　　　DOMESMONT.

　　　　　Bde. H.Q......RIBEAUCOURT.

180 Bde.　　　　　　 180 Inf. Bde.　　　)MEZEROLLES (S. of river)
Area.　　　　　　　　1/6 Fd. Co. R.E.)LE MEILLARD-HEUZECOURT
　　　　　　　　　　　2/6 Fd. Amb.　　　)BERNAVILLE-VACQUERIE-GORGES
　　　　　　　　　　　Det. Train.　　　　)BERNEUIL.

　　　　　Bde. H.Q......BERNAVILLE.

181 Bde.　　　　　　 181 Inf. Bde.　　　) OCCOCHES Fm. OUTREBOIS(S.
Area.　　　　　　　　3/3 Fd. Co.R.E.) of river) BOISBERGUES
　　　　　　　　　　　1/12 L.N.Lancs. R.) AUTHEUX-FIENVILLERS.
　　　　　　　　　　　2/6 Fd. Amb.　　　) CANDAS will be added to this
　　　　　　　　　　　Det. Train.　　　　) area after 9.30 a.m. on
　　　　　　　　　　　　　　　　　　　　　　30th October.

　　　　　Bde. H.Q......FIENVILLERS.

2. Refilling Point: Road between BERNAVILLE and FIENVILLERS.

3. Div. H.Q. will be at BERNAVILLE.

4. Acknowledge.

Issued at.......　　　　　　　　　　　　　　　　(signed)
　　　　　　　　　　　　　　　　　　　　　　　　Lieut-Colonel,
Copies to:　　　　　　　　　　　　　　　　　　　General Staff.
　A.D.C. (for G.O.C.)
　179 Inf. Bde.　　　　　　　　　Div. Train.
　180 Inf. Bde.　　　　　　　　　Div. Supply Column.
　181 Inf. Bde.　　　　　　　　　A.D.V.S.
　C.R.A.　　　　　　　　　　　　　Camp Commandant.
　C.R.E.　　　　　　　　　　　　　3rd Army.
　"A".　　　　　　　　　　　　　　IV Corps.
　A.D.M.S.　　　　　　　　　　　　War Diary.
　Signals.　　　　　　　　　　　　File.
　1/12 L.N.Lancs R.

SECRET.

War Diary

General Staff Branch - 60th Div. H.Q.

Vol 6

1 - 30th Nov. 1916.

From: 1st Nov. 1916.

Army Form C. 2118.

WAR DIARY
or
INTELLIGENCE SUMMARY
(Erase heading not required.)

Instructions regarding War Diaries and Intelligence Summaries are contained in F.S. Regs., Part II. and the Staff Manual respectively. Title Pages will be prepared in manuscript.

Place	Date	Hour	Summary of Events and Information	Remarks and references to Appendices
BERNAVILLE	1st	9.15 p.m	Operation Orders 7.8.9 issued for move of Div to new area. Weather wet. Wind S.W.	Ops App. A.
"	2nd		Civ. C. inspected various units of this Division and saw Brigadiers during the afternoon. Weather fair. Wind S.W. Division still training in G.H.Q. Reserve.	
AILLY LE HAUT CLOCHER	3rd	10 a.m.	Divisional H.Q. established AILLY LE HAUT CLOCHER. App 180 All units moving to new area. Weather fair. Wind S.W.	
"	4th		Division completed the move to new area and commenced reorganization. Weather fair. Wind S.W.	
"	5th		Division continues reorganization. Training carried out. Weather stormy. Southerly gale.	
"	6th		Division continues reorganization. Training carried out. Weather fair. Strong wind S.W.	
"	7th		Division continues reorganization. Training carried out. Weather fair, wet. Strong wind S.W.	
"	8th		Division continues reorganization. Training carried out. Weather fair. Wind S.W.	
"	9th		Division continues reorganization. Training carried out. Weather fair. Wind W.	
"	10th		Division continues reorganization. Training carried out. Weather fine. Slight breeze.	

Army Form C. 2118.

WAR DIARY
or
INTELLIGENCE SUMMARY

(Erase heading not required.)

Instructions regarding War Diaries and Intelligence Summaries are contained in F. S. Regs., Part II. and the Staff Manual respectively. Title Pages will be prepared in manuscript.

Place	Date	Hour	Summary of Events and Information	Remarks and references to Appendices
AILLY LE HAUT CLOCHER.	11		Division continued reorganization. Training carried out. Weather fine, wind slight W. Misty.	CRS
"	12		Division continued reorganization. Training carried out. Weather fine, wind slight W.	CRS
"	13		Division continued reorganization. Training carried out. Operation Order No 10 issued. Weather fair but misty, wind slight W.	CRS App. B / CRS
"	14		Division continued reorganization. Training carried out. Division Commander entrainment at LONGPRÉ. Weather fair, wind slight W.	CRS / CRS
"	15		Division continues reorganization and entrainment. Training carried out. Weather fair and cold. Wind N.E. Operation Order No 11 and amendment issued	CRS / CRS / CRS App. C
"	16		Division continues reorganization and entrainment. Training carried out. Weather fair & cold. Wind N.E.	CRS / CRS
"	17		Division continues reorganization and entrainment. Training carried out. G/S 4.27 issued with programme of entrainment. Wind strong S.E.	CRS App. D / CRS
"	18		Division continues reorganization and entrainment. Training carried out. G.S. 428 issued with programme of entrainment. Weather fair re'ed. Wind strong S.E.	CRS App. E / CRS
"	19		Division continues reorganization and entrainment. Training carried out. Weather fair, wind	CRS / CRS

Army Form C. 2118.

WAR DIARY
or
INTELLIGENCE SUMMARY

(Erase heading not required.)

Instructions regarding War Diaries and Intelligence Summaries are contained in F.S. Regs., Part II. and the Staff Manual respectively. Title Pages will be prepared in manuscript.

Place	Date	Hour	Summary of Events and Information	Remarks and references to Appendices
AILLY LE HAUT CLOCHER.	20		Division continues reorganisation and entrainment. Training carried out. Weather fair. Wind S.E. G/S 429 issued.	
"	21		Division continues reorganisation and entrainment. Training carried out. Weather fair. Wind S.E. G/S 431 issued.	App. F App. F
"	22		Division continues reorganisation and entrainment. Training carried out. Weather fine. Wind S.E.	App. G
"	23		Division continues reorganisation and entrainment. Weather fine. Wind S.E.	App. H
"	24		Division continues reorganisation and entrainment. Div. H.Q. entrains.	
"	25		Division completed entrainment.	
"	26		Division in process of move to M by sea and land.	
MARSEILLES	27		Div. H.Q. established at MARSEILLES. Division in process of move.	
"	28		Division in process of move.	
"	29		Division in process of move.	
"	30		Division in process of move. Div. H.Q. Embarked on S.S. IVERNIA.	

1. XII. 1916.

[signature]
60th Division

APPENDIX "A"

War Diary

Copy No. 31

SECRET.

60th DIVISION ORDER No. 5.

Ref. Map. LENS Sheet 11 and
ABBEVILLE Sheet 14, 1/100,000.

November 1st 1916.

1. The Division will halt for the night 3/4 November as under :-

Designation of Area.	Troops.	Area.
Div. H.Q. Area.	Div. H.Q. 60 San. Sec. 60 Mob. Vet. Sec. Det. Train.	) AILLY LE HAUT CLOCHER -) FAMECHON.
179 Bde. Area.	179 Inf. Bde. 2/4 Fd. Co. R.E. 2/4 Fd. Amb. Det. Train.	) VAUCHELLES LES QUESNOY -) BELLANCOURT - EAUCOURT SUR) SOMME - FRANCIERES -) BUIGNY L'ABBE.
	H.Q.	BELLANCOURT.
180 Bde. Area.	180 Inf. Bde. 1/6 Fd. Co. R.E. 2/5 Fd. Amb. Det. Train.	) BUSSUS-BUSSUE - YAUCOURT -) BUSSUS - ALLIEL -) GORENFLOS.
	H.Q.	GORENFLOS.
181 Bde. Area.	181 Inf. Bde. 3/3 Fd.Co.R.E. 2/6 Fd.Amb. Det.Train.	) CANDAS - FIENVILLERS -) GORGES - BERNEUIL -) ST. HILAIRE.
	H.Q.	FIENVILLERS.
Pioneer Area.	1/12 L.N.Lancs.R.	) RIBEAUCOURT and DOMESMONT.

2. Refilling Points will remain unchanged.

3. Div. H.Q. will be at AILLY LE HAUT CLOCHER.

4. Acknowledge.

T. Humphreys
Lieut-Colonel,
General Staff.

Issued at 9-15 p.m.
Copies to :-
A.D.C. for G.O.C.
179 Inf. Bde.
180 Inf. Bde.
181 Inf. Bde.
C.R.A.
C.R.E.
"A"
A.D.M.S.
Signals.
1/12 L.N.Lancs.

Div. Train.
Div. Supply Column.
A.D.V.S.
Camp Commandant.
Vth Army.
IVth Corps.
IVth Army.
XVth Corps.
War Diary.
File.

APPENDIX "A"

SECRET.   Copy No. ....

60th DIVISION ORDER NO. 7.

Ref. Map LENS Sheet 11 - ABBEVILLE Sheet 14, 1/100,000.   November 1st 1918.

1. The Division will move westwards on the 3rd November as under:-

Group.	Troops.	Starting Point.	Time.
A.	Div. H.Q.	Road junction at South western	9.40a.m.
	60 San.Sec.	end of BERNAVILLE, north of	9.50a.m.
	60 Mob.Vet. Sec.	first E in Pt.VACQUERIE.	9.50a.m.

Route : RIBEAUCOURT - FRANSU - ERGNIES.

B.	H.Q.,179 Inf.Bde.	Road junction just N. of F	10.30a.m.
	179 M.G.Co.	of FRANQUEVILLE.	10.30a.m.
	179 T.M.Batty.		10.30a.m.
	2/16 Lond. R.		10.40a.m.
	2/15 Lond. R.		10.50a.m.

Route : ERGNIES - AILLY LE HAUT CLOCHER.

	2/13 Lond. R.	Road junction just N.W. of	9.15a.m.
	2/14 Lond. R.	B of BEAUMETZ	9.25a.m.
	2/4 Fd.Co.R.E.		9.35a.m.
	2/4 Fd.Amb.		9.40a.m.

Route : ... ... ST. RIQUIER.

C.	H.Q. 180 Inf.Bde.	Road junction N.W. of S	10.40.a.m
	180 T.M.Batty.	in LONGVILLERS.	10.40.a.m
	2/17 Lond.R.		11. 0.a.m
	2/20 Lond.R.		11.10.a.m.
	1/6 Fd.Co.R.E.		11.20.a.m.
	2/5 Fd.Amb.		11.25.a.m.

Route : LONGVILLERS - DOMQUEUR.

	2/19 Lond. R.	Road junction just East of	8.30a.m.
	180 M.G.Co.	E of ST. HILAIRE.	8.40a.m.
	2/18 Lond. R.		8.45a.m.

Route : DOMART EN PONTHIEU - GORENFLOS.

D.	2/21 Lond. R.	Cross-roads just W. of A	10. a.m.
	181 M.G.Co.	of AUTHEUX.	10.10a.m.
	181 T.M.Batty.		10.10a.m.
	3/3 Fd.Co.R.E.		10.20a.m.
	2/6 Fd.Amb.		10.25a.m.

Route : FIENVILLERS - BERNEUIL.

E.	1/12 L.N.Lancs.R.	Road junction at Western end of BOISBERGUES.	10. a.m.

Route : BERNAVILLE - RIBEAUCOURT.

2. A distance of 100 yards is to be maintained between units.

3. Baggage wagons will accompany their units.

4. Troops not mentioned in above will remain in their present billets.

5. Div. H.Q. will close at BERNAVILLE at 9.30a.m. and open at AILLY LE HAUT CLOCHER at the same hour.

6. Acknowledge.

E.T. Humphreys
Lieut-Colonel,
General Staff.

Issued at 9-15p

Copies to :

A.D.C. for G.O.C.	"A".		
179 Inf. Bde.	A.D.M.S.	A.D.V.S.	XVth Corps.
180 Inf. Bde.	Signals.	Camp Commandant.	War Diary.
181 Inf. Bde.	1/12 L.N.Lancs.R.	Vth Army.	File.
C.R.A.	Div. Train.	IVth Corps.	
C.R.E.	Div. Supply Col.	IVth Army.	

APPENDIX 'A'

War Diary
21

SECRET.　　　　　　　　　　　　　　　　　　　　　　COPY NO. 21.

60th DIVISION ORDER NO. 9

November 1st 1916.

Ref.Map LENS Sheet 11 and
　　　　ABBEVILLE Sheet 14, 1/100,000.

1. The troops mentioned below will move westwards on the 4th

　November as under :-

Group.	Troops.	Starting Point.	Time.
A.	1/12 L.N.Lancs R.	Road junction in RIBEAUCOURT.	10a.m.
	Route : ERGNIES.		
B.	181 Inf.Bde.	Road junction ¼-mile	10a.m.
	3/3 Fd.Co.R.E.	S. of ST. HILAIRE	10.40a.m.
	2/6 Fd.Amb.	CHURCH.	10.45a.m.
	Route : DOMART EN PONTHIEU.		

2. Baggage Wagons will accompany their units.

3. A distance of 100 yds. will be maintained between units.

4. The troops mentioned above will halt for the night 4/5th

　November as under :-

Designation of Area.	Troops.	Area.
Div.H.Q. Area.	1/12 L.N.Lancs.R.	AILLY LE HAUT CLOCHER.
181 Bde.Area.	181 Inf.Bde.	ERGNIES - VILLERS SOUS
	3/3 Fd.Co.R.E.	AILLY - MOUFLERS.
	2/6 Fd.Amb.	VAUCHELLES LES DOMART.
	Det. Train.	BRUCAMPS.
H.Q.	... BRUCAMPS.	

5. Refilling Points. ABBEVILLE - FLIXECOURT Road just West and
　　　　　　　　　　　South-east of AILLY LE HAUT CLOCHER.

6. Div. H.Q. will be at AILLY LE HAUT CLOCHER.

7. Acknowledge.

　　　　　　　　　　　　　　　　　　　　E.T. Humphreys.
Issued at 9-15 p.m.　　　　　　　　　　　Lieut-Colonel,
　　　　　　　　　　　　　　　　　　　　General Staff.

Copies to :-

A.D.C. for G.O.C.　　　　　　Div. Train.
179 Inf. Bde.　　　　　　　　Div. Supply Column.
180 Inf. Bde.　　　　　　　　A.D.V.S.
181 Inf. Bde.　　　　　　　　Camp Commandant.
C.R.A.　　　　　　　　　　　Vth Army.
C.R.E.　　　　　　　　　　　IVth Corps.
"A"　　　　　　　　　　　　IVth Army.
A.D.M.S.　　　　　　　　　　XVth Corps.
Signals.　　　　　　　　　　War Diary.
1/12 L.N.Lancs.　　　　　　　File.

APPENDIX 'B'

War Diary 19

SECRET.   60th. Division Order No. 10.   Copy No........

November 13th. 1916.

Ref. map LENS Sheet 11, ABBEVILLE Sheet /14, &
AMIENS Sheet 17. 1/100,000.

1. The Division will move to entraining station at LONGPRÉ and
commence to move Southwards as under:-

14th. November. 1916.

UNIT.	Starting Point.	TIME OF PASSING S.P.	ROUTE.
2/4th.Fd.Amb.	Cross roads BEAUCOURT SUR SOMME.	11-40 a.m.	PONT REMY-LIERCOURT-FONTAINE.
Det.Div.Amm. Col.	Crossroads just W. of P. of PONT REMY.	12-45 p.m.	LIERCOURT-FONTAINE.
Det.2/15th.Bn. Lond. R.	Crossroads FRANCIERES.	3-40 p.m.	JOCQUEREL-FONTAINE.
Det.Div.Amm. Col.	Crossroads just W. of P. of PONT REMY.	4. p.m.	LIERCOURT-FONTAINE.
2/4th.Fd. Co. R.E.	Crossroads BEAUCOURT SUR SOMME.	6. p.m.	PONT REMY-LIERCOURT-FONTAINE.
302nd.Bde.Amm. Col.	Crossroads BOURDON.	6-25 p.m.	HANGEST SUR SOMME-CONDE.

15th. November 1916.

UNIT.	Starting Point.	TIME OF PASSING S.P.	ROUTE.
One Baty. 302nd. R.F.A.Bde.	Crossroads BOURDON.	12-30 a.m.	HANGEST SUR SOMME-CONDE.
H.Q.179th.Inf. Bde.179th.T.M. Bty.	Crossroads just S.W. of B. of BELLANCOURT.	11-30 p.m. (14th.Nov.)	PONT REMY-LIERCOURT-FONTAINE.
180th.T.M.Bty.	Road junction just S.E. of GORENFLOS.	12-5 a.m.	BRUCAMPS-VAUCHELLES LES DOMART-LA FOLIE L'ETOILE-CONDE.
H.Q. & 1.Bty. 302nd.R.F.A. Bde.	Crossroads BOURDON.	4 a.m.	HANGEST SUR SOMME-CONDE.
Det.2/15th.Bn. Lond.R.	Crossroads FRANCIERES.	4 a.m.	JOCQUEREL FONTAINE.
2/16th.Lond.R.	Crossroads just S.W. of B. of BELLANCOURT.	6 a.m.	PONT REMY-LIERCOURT-FONTAINE.
Det.2/15th.Bn. Lond. R.	Crossroads FRANCIERES.	7-30 a.m.	JOCQUEREL-FONTAINE.
Det.2/15th.Bn. Lond. R.	Crossroads FRANCIERES.	1 p.m.	JOCQUEREL-FONTAINE.
2/13th.Lond.R.	Road junction just W. of V of VAUCHELLES.	11-40 a.m.	PONT REMY-LIERCOURT-FONTAINE.
2/14th.Lond.R.	Road junction S. end of BUIGNY L'ABBE.	2-30 p.m.	PONT REMY-LIERCOURT-FONTAINE.
Det.2/15th.Bn. Lond. R.	Crossroads FRANCIERES.	4-25 p.m.	JOCQUEREL-FONTAINE.

2. The 60th.Amm. Sub-Park will entrain at LONGEAU at 3 p.m. 15th.inst.
and will leave EPAGNE at 7-30 a.m.

Route:- L'ETOILE-FLIXECOURT-BELLOY SUR SOMME-PICQUIGNY-AMIENS.

It must allow any troops of the Division crossing ITS route

between EAUCOURT SUR SOMME and COCQUEREL (both inclusive) to pass through.

3. All units of the Division not mentioned above will remain in their present billets.

Issued at 4.p.m.

A. Bolton Captain G.S.
for Lieut.Colonel,
General Staff.

Copies to:-

A.D.C.for G.O.C.
179th.Inf.Bde.
180th.   ,,
181st.   ,,
C.R.A.
C.R.E.
"A"
A.D.M.S.
Signals.
60th.Amm.Sub-Park.

Div.Train.
Div.Supply Column.
A.D.V.S.
Camp Commandant.
IVth.Army.
XVth.Corps.
War Diary.
File.

APPENDIX 'C'

War Diary
20

SECRET.

60th Division Order No 11.

Copy No 20

November 15th, 1916

Ref.Map LENS Sheet 11, ABBEVILLE Sheet 14, & AMIENS Sheet 17. 1/100,000.

1. The Division will continue to move Southwards on 16th & 17th November, in accordance with attached programme of entrainment and Schedule "A".

2. All units of the Division not mentioned in the attached programme of entrainment will remain in their present billets.

3. Acknowledge.

Issued at 11 a.m.

C.A.Bolton Captain GS
for Lieut.Colonel,
General Staff.

Copies to

A.D.C. for G.O.C.
179th Inf.Bde.
179th M.G.Coy.
180th Inf.Bde.
181st " "
C.R.A.
C.R.E.
"A"
A.D.M.S.
Signals.

60th Amn.Sub-Park.
Div.Train.
Div.Supply Column.
A.D.V.S.
Camp Commandant.
IVth Army.
XVth Corps.
War Diary.
File.

SECRET

TABLE OF PERSONNEL, ANIMALS & VEHICLES

Proceeding on the 16th & 17th Nov.

SCHEDULE "A"

—* 16th.November.*—

No. of Train.	Type of Train.	Time of Departure.	Unit.	Officers	Other Ranks	Animals	Vehicles 4 wheeled.	Vehicles 2 wheeled.
9th.	T.C.	10-27 a.m.	Part One Batty. } 302nd.R.F.A.Bde.} Det.Div.Amn.Col.	4.	120.	135.	1.	26.
10th.	T.C.	2-17 p.m.	Part One Batty. } 302nd.R.F.A.Bde.} Det.Div.Amn.Col.	1. 4.	60. 120.	95. 135.	1.	30. 26.
11th.	T.P.	5-27 p.m.	Part of above two Batteries 302nd. R.F.A.Bde. 181st.T.M.Batty. No.2.Sec.Div.Signals. *Small Arms Section Amn. Col.	2. 2. 4. 1. 3.	60. 40. 46. 27. 255.	95. — 10. 25.	2.	30. 84.

*or Det. of a Bn.
180th.Inf.Bde.of approx. same strength.

—* 17th.November.*—

No. of Train.	Type of Train.	Time of Departure.	Unit.	Officers	Other Ranks	Animals	Vehicles 4 wheeled.	Vehicles 2 wheeled.
12th.	T.C.	10-27a.m.	Det.Div.Amn.Col.	3. 5.	100. 5.	255.		56.
13th.	Special.	2-17p.m.	Det.2/17th.Lond.R. Det.Div.Amn.Col. Det.2/17th.Lond.R.	2. 5. 2.	140. 5. 200.	376.		
14th.	T.C.	5-27p.m.	Det.Div.Amn.Col. Det.Div.Train. Det.2/17th.Lond.R.	2. 2. 19.	100. 308. 182.	24.		36. 20.
15th.	Special	9-27p.m.	179th.M.G.Co. Det.Div.Train. Det.2/17th.Lond.R.	10. 2. 10.	50. 340.	10. 92.		

	1st.Class.	Covered Trucks.	Flat Trucks.	Brake Vans.
Types of Trains. T.C. = Type combatant. composed of	1.	33.	14.	2.
T.P. = Type Pare, composed of	1.	24.	23.	2.
Special = Composed of	1.	47.	2.	2

S E C R E T.

PROGRAM OF ENTRAINMENT.

16th November, 1916.

UNIT.	Starting point.	Time of start.	Route to Station.	Time due at Stn.	Entrain- ing Stn.	Time of depart- ure of train.
Pt. of 1 Btty. 302 Bde. R.F.A.	BOURDON Cross Roads.	5-30 a.m.	HANGEST-sur- SOMME - CONDE.	7-27 a.m.	LONGPRE	10-27 a.m.
Det. Divl. Amn. Col.	Cross Roads just W. of P. of PONT REMY	4-30 a.m.	LIERCOURT- FONTAINE.	"	"	"
Pt. of 1 Btty. 302 Bde. R.F.A.	BOURDON Cross Roads.	9-15 a.m.	HANGEST-sur- SOMME - CONDE.	11-17 a.m.	"	2-17 p.m.
Det. Divl. Amn. Col.	Cross Roads just W. of PONT REMY	8-15 a.m.	LIERCOURT- FONTAINE.	"	"	"
Remdr. of above 2 Bttys. 302nd Bde, R.F.A.	BOURDON Cross Roads.	(Those portions must go with remainder of their Batteries to the Station and remain there until due for entrain- ment.)		2-27 p.m.	"	5-27 p.m.
181 T.M.Btty.	Cross Roads ERUCAMPS.	12-15 p.m.	VAUCHELLES-les- DOMART-LA FOLIE- L'ETOILE-CONDE.	"	"	"
No.2 Sec.Div. Signal Coy.	Cross Roads just S.W. of B. of BELLAN- COURT.	11-20 a.m.	PONT REMY- LIERCOURT- PONT REM.	"	"	"
Small Arms Sec. Amn. Col. ✗	BOURDON Cross Roads.	12-30 p.m.	HANGEST-sur- SOMME - CONDE.	"	"	"
or ✗ Det.of a Batt. 180 Inf. Bde.	"	"	"	"	"	"

✗ If the S.A. Section, Ammunition Column is available, it will proceed, otherwise the detachment of a Battalion, 180th Inf. Bde. will move. Instructions will be issued as soon as possible as to which is to go by the train. The time of starting and route will be arranged by the 180th Inf. Bde., should their detachment go, and the Divisional H'qrs must be informed.

(1)

S E C R E T.

PROGRAMME OF ENTRAINMENT.

17th November, 1916.

Unit.	Starting point.	Time of start.	Route to station.	Entraining stn.	Time due at stn.	Time of departure of train.
Det. Divl. Amm. Col.	Cross Roads just W. of P of Pont REMY.	5-0 a.m.	LIERCOURT-FONTAINE.	LONGPRE.	7-27 a.m.	10-27 a.m.
Det.2/17th Bn.Lond.R.	Road junction in BUSSUS BUSSUEL leading to AILLY.	-	AILLY-le-HAUT CLOCHER-LONG.	"	"	"
Det. Divl. Amm. Col.	Cross Roads just W. of P of PONT REMY.	9 a.m.	LIERCOURT-FONTAINE.	"	?	"
Det. 2/17th Bn. Lond. R.	Road junction in BUSSUS BUSSUEL leading to AILLY.	-	AILLY-le-HAUT CLOCHER-LONG.	"	11-17 a.m.	2-17 p.m.
Det. Divl. Amm. Col.	Cross Roads just W. of P of PONT REMY.	12 noon.	LIERCOURT-FONTAINE.	"	"	"
Det.Divl. Train.	Road junction Western end of YZEUX.	12-15 p.m.	BOURDON-HANGEST-sur-SOMME-CONDE.	"	2-27 p.m.	5-27 p.m.
Det. 2/17th Bn. Lond. R.	Road junction in BUSSUS BUSSUEL leading to AILLY.	11-40 a.m.	AILLY-le-HAUT CLOCHER-LONG.	"	"	"
Det. 2/17th Bn. Lond. R.	-do-	3-40 p.m.	-do-	"	"	"
179 M.G. Coy.	Road junction just E. of V of VAUCHELLES.	2-15 p.m.	PONT REMY-LIERCOURT-FONTAINE.	"	6-27 p.m.	9-27 p.m.
Det. Divl. Train.	Road junction Western end of YZEUX.	-	BOURDON-HANGEST-sur-SOMME-CONDE.	"	"	"

× Those parties can move under Bde. arrangements but must arrive at entraining station 1½ hours before departure of train.

APPENDIX 'C'.

War Diary

SECRET.   COPY NO......
           SCHEDULE "A" AND PROGRAMME OF ENTRAINMENT 16th.Nov.1916.
           Following amendments to
           issued with 60th.Div.Order.No.11 are to be inserted in all copies.

                    -*- SCHEDULE "A".-*-

1. 9th.Train first line 5 officers 140 other ranks instead of 4 officers 120 other ranks.
          third line 1   "   40   "   "   "   1   "   60   "   "
10th. "   first line 5   "   140   "   "   "   4   "   120   "   "
          third line 1   "   40   "   "   "   1   "   60   "   "
11th. "   first line Det.Div.Arr.Col. instead of "Part of above 2 Batteries 302nd.R.F.A.Bde.
          consisting of 1 officer 40 other ranks,No animals,No 4 wheeled vehicles, 60.-2 wheel-
          INSTEAD OF... 2 officers 40   "   "   "   NO   "   "   2-4   "   84.-2   "

                    -*- PROGRAMME OF ENTRAINMENT.-*-
                          16th.November.1916.

FIFTH HORIZONTAL DETAIL.
UNIT.   STARTING   TIME OF   ROUTE TO   ENTRAINING   TIME DUE   TIME OF DEPARTURE
         POINT.   START.   STATION.   STATION.   AT STN.   OF TRAIN.

Det.Divl. Cross Rds   12 Noon.   LIERCOURT-   LONGPRE.   2-27 p.m.   5-27 p.m.
Arr.Col. just W. of   FONTAINE.
         P of PONT
         REMY.

INSTEAD OF:-

Remdr.of BOURDON) Those portions must go with   -do-   -do-   -do-
above 2. cross Rds) the remainder of their
Battys.   ) Batt,ries to the Station
302nd.Bde.   ) and remain there until due
R.F.A.   ) for entrainment.

                                                   Signed
                                                   Captain.G.S.
                                                   for Lieut.Col.,
                                                   General Staff.

APPENDIX "D"

G/S.427.

A.D.C. for G.O.C.   Div. Train.
179 M.G.Co.   Div. Supply Column.
180 Inf.Bde.   A.D.V.S.
181 Inf. Bde.   Camp Commandant.
C.R.A.   IVth Army.
C.R.E.   XVth Corps.
"A".   War Diary.
A.D.M.S.   File.
Signals.

---

         and 19th
Units will entrain on 18th/November 1916 in accordance with attached Schedule "A" and Programme of Entrainment.

Acknowledge.

C.A. Bolton.
Captain.
General Staff.
60th Division.

16/11/16.

SECRET.

COPY NO. .....
SCHEDULE "A".

Table of Personnel, Animals and Vehicles proceeding on the 18th and 19th November 1915.

18th November 1915.

No. of Train.	Type of Train.	Time of Departure.	Unit.	Officers.	Other Ranks.	Animals.	Vehicles.	Covered Trucks.	Flat Trucks
16	T.C.	10.27 a.m.	H.Q. 1/6 Div. R.F.A.	1	57	102	12	5	14
17	Special.	2.17 p.m.	Det. 1/6 Fd. Co. R.E. Part of 301 R.F.A. Bde. Amn. Col. 2/19 Lond.R.	5 2 5 3	120 90 958 115	24 23	2 20	26 4	25
18	T.C.	5.27 p.m.	Det. 1/5 Fd. Co. R.E. Amn. Col. 301 R.F.A. Bde. Ken. 2/5 Fd. Amb. Det. 2/5 Fd. Amb.	39 1 8 5	120 48 289 200	45 67 53	3 1	14 34	
19	Special.	9.27 p.m.	H.Q. Div.Train. Det. 180 Inf. Bde. H.Q. 2/20 Lond.R.	7 39	40 958	20 24	2 1		

19th November 1915.

No. of Train.	Type of Train.	Time of Departure.	Unit.	Officers.	Other Ranks.	Animals.	Vehicles.	Covered Trucks.	Flat Trucks
20	T.C.	10.27 a.m.	H.Q. 301 R.F.A. Bde. One battery 301 R.F.A. Bde. H.Q. Div. R.A. One Battery 301 R.F.A. Bde.	5 5 2 5	49 140 17 140	48 135 23 145	1 1 1	26 4 24	
21	T.C.	5.27 p.m.	Det. 35th Cas. Clearing Stn. X.60 T.M.Battery. H.Q. Div. Sig. Co.	11 2 1	81 25 59	33	2		

Types of Trains.
T.C. = Type Combatant, composed of.....
T.P. = Type Parc, composed of.....
Special. = Composed of........

SECRET.

COPY NO............

Ref. Map: EMS Sheet 11. AMIENS Sheet 17.
ABBEVILLE Sheet 14. 1/100,000.

PROGRAMME OF ENTRAINMENT.

18th November 1916.

Unit.	Starting Point.	Time of Starting.	Route to Station.	Entraining Station.	Time of departure of train
H.Q. Div. R.E. Det. 1/6 Fd. Co. R.E.	AILLY LE HAUT CLOCHER Crossroads. Crossroads BUSSUS BUSSUEL	3.55 a.m. 4.10 a.m.	LONG - LE CATELET. AILLY - LE CATELET.	LONGPRE.	7.27 a.m. 10.27 a.m.
Part 301 R.F.A. Bde. Amm. Col.	Crossroads N. of BETHENCOURT.	4.30 a.m.	LE CATELET FLIXECOURT - CONDE.	"	"
2/19 Lond.R.	AILLY LE HAUT CLOCHER Crossroads.	9.30 a.m.	LONG - LE CATELET.	"	11.17 a.m.
Rem. 1/6 Fd. Co. R.E.	Crossroads BUSSUS BUSSUEL.	8.35 a.m.	AILLY - LONG - LE CATELET.	"	2.17 p.m.
Det. 2/5 Fd. Amb.	"	8.25 a.m.	"	"	"
Rem. 301 R.F.A.	Crossroads N. of BETHENCOURT.	11.30 a.m.	FLIXECOURT - CONDE.	"	5.27 p.m.
Bde. Amm. Col. Rem. 2/5 Fd. Amb.	Crossroads BUSSUS BUSSUEL.	11.40 a.m.	AILLY - LONG - LE CATELET.	"	2.27 p.m.
Det. Div. Train. (To be arranged by O.C. Div. Train.)					
H.Q. 180 Inf.Bde.	Road junction S.E. end of GORENFLOS.	4.10 p.m.	BRUCAMPS - VAUCHELLES - L'ETOILE	"	6.27 p.m.
2/20 Lond.R.	Crossroads YAUCOURT BUSSUS.	3.50 p.m.	AILLY - LONG LE CATELET.	"	9.27 p.m.

***** 19th November 1916. *****

H.Q. 301 R.F.A. Bde.	Crossroads ?. of BETHENCOURT.	4.30 a.m.	FLIXECOURT - CONDE.	"	7.27 a.m.
One battery 301 R.F.A. Bde.	Road junction S. end of AILLY.	6.0 a.m.	LONG - LE CATELET.	"	"
One batty. 301 R.F.A.	Crossroads N. of BETHENCOURT.	11.30 a.m.	FLIXECOURT - CONDE.	"	2.27 p.m.
A.E.A. Bde.					
Det. 55 Cas. Clearing Station.	AILLY LE HAUT CLOCHER Crossroads.	12.40 p.m.	LONG - LE CATELET.	"	5.27 p.m.
X.60 Div. Sig. Co.	"	12.45 p.m.	"	"	"
X.60 T.M. battery.	Crossroads just W. of PONT REMY.	Noon.	LIERCOURT PONT REMY.	"	"

The following :-T. will also entrain on the 19th November 1916. Orders will be issued, a regards those, later.

Det. 55 Cas. Clearing Station. Drivers Lorries.
Rem. 60th Amm. Sub. Park.   6   3
Det. 60 Div. Supply Column.   30   12
                                  40   18.

APPENDIX E.

SECRET.   G/S.428/1.

A.D.C. for G.O.C.   Div. Train.
180 Inf. Bde.   Div. Supply Column.
181 Inf. Bde.   A.D.V.S.
C.R.A.   Camp Commandant.
C.R.E.   IVth Army.
"A".   XVth Corps.
A.D.M.S.   35 Cas. Clearing Station.
Signals.   War Diary.
                           File.

The following amendments to Programme of
Entrainment for 20th and 21st should be made in all copies.

In 22nd Train.

    For "No. 2 Sec. Div. Sig. Co.",
    read "No. 3 Sec Div. Sig. Co.".

In 24th Train.

    For "One battery 303 R.F.A. Bde.",
    read "One battery 301 R.F.A. Bde."

and, under "Starting Point"

    For "Road junction just W. of BELLOY sur SOMME",
    read "Crossroads S.W. End of BETHENCOURT."

                                                  Captain.
                                            General Staff.
18/11/16.   60th Division.

APPENDIX "E"

SECRET.   COPY NO. 18
                                                                G/S.428.

A.D.C. for G.O.C.   Div. Train.
180 Inf. Bde.   Div. Supply Column.
181 Inf. Bde.   A.D.V.S.
C.R.A.   Camp Commandant.
C.R.E.   IVth Army.
"A".   XVth Corps.
A.D.M.S.   35 Cas. Clearing Stn.
Signals.   War Diary.

Units will entrain on 20th / and 21st November 1916 in accordance with attached Schedule "A" and Programme of Entrainment. The times of starting are provisional, on the understanding that previous trains leave up to scheduled time. They will be adhered to, unless orders to the contrary are issued.

Acknowledge.

                                          G. Bolton.
                                                Captain.
                                                General Staff.
18/11/16.   60th Division.

SECRET.

COPY No. 18
SCHEDULE A.

Table of Personnel, Animals & Vehicles proceeding on the 20th/21st November 1916.

November 20th 1916.

No. of Train.	Type of Train.	Time of Departure.	Unit.	Officers.	Other Ranks.	Animals.	Vehicles 4 w.	Vehicles 2 w.
22	Special.	10.27 a.m.	2/18 Lond.R.(less 1 Co & Det.)	26	693	-	-	-
23	T.C.	5.27 p.m.	180 M.G. Co. (less Det.)	8	178	10	-	-
			302 S.A.A. Sec. Amn. Col.	3	255	25	-	-
			No. 2 Sec. Div. Sig. Co.	1	27	10	-	-
			No. 1 Sec. Div. Sig. Co.	2	71	45	4	-
			One Battery 301 R.F.A. Bde.	5	140	135	1	26
			Det. Div. Train.	1	24	20	-	8
			Det. 2/18 Lond.R.	10	10	-	-	-
			Det. 180 M.G. Co.	4	4	-	-	-

***** November 21st 1916. *****

No. of Train.	Type of Train.	Time of Departure.	Unit.	Officers.	Other Ranks.	Animals.	Vehicles 4 w.	Vehicles 2 w.
24	T.C.	10.27 a.m.	One Battery 303 R.F.A. Bde.	5	140	135	1	26
			Det. Div. Train.	4	150	49	-	13
25	T.C.	5.27 p.m.	One Battery 303 R.F.A. Bde.	5	140	135	1	25
			Det. Div. Train.	4	150	49	-	13

Types of Trains. T.C. = Type Combatant, composed of ....
T.P. = Type Parc, composed of ....
Special. = Composed of ....

	1st Class.	Covered Trucks.	Flat Trucks.
	1	33	14
	1	24	23
	1	47	

SECRET.   COPY NO. 18.

PROGRAMME OF ENTRAINMENT.

Ref. Map: LENS Sheet 11. AMIENS Sheet 17. ABBEVILLE Sheet 14. 1/100,000.

20th November 1916.

Unit.	Starting Point.	Time of Starting.	Route to Station.	Entraining Station.	Time due at Station.	Time of departure of train.
2/18 Lond.R. (less Dets.)	Road junction S.E. end of GORENFLOS.	5 a.m.	BRUCAMPS - VAUCHELLES - LA FOLIE - L'ETOILE - CONDE.	LONGPRE.	7.27 a.m.	10.27 a.m.
180 ..G. Co. (less Det.)	"	"	"	"	"	"
No. 2 Sec. Div. Sig. Co.	"	5.10 a.m.	"	"	"	"
302 Sp.A. Sec. Amm. Col.	BOUFFON Crossroads.	5.45 a.m.	HANGEST - CONDE.	"	"	"
No. 1 Sec. Div. Sig. Co.	Crossroads AILLY LE HAUT CLOCHER.	12.10 p.m.	LONG - LE CATELET.	"	2.27 p.m.	5.27 p.m.
One Battery 301 Bde. R.F.A.	Crossroads S.E. end of BETHENCOURT.	12 noon.	FLIXECOURT - CONDE.	"	"	"
Det. Div. Train.	(To be arranged by O.C., Div. Train).					
Det. 2/18 Lond.R. Det. 180 M.G.Co.	(These parties can proceed to the station under arrangements of the 180th Inf. Bde.) (They must be at Station 1½ hours before train is due to start.)					

21st November 1916.

Unit.	Starting Point.	Time of Starting.	Route to Station.	Entraining Station.	Time due at Station.	Time of departure of train.
One Battery 303 Bde. R.F.A.	Road junction just W. of BELLOY sur SOMME.	4.40 a.m.	BOURDON - HANGEST - CONDE.	LONGPRE.	7.27 a.m.	10.27 a.m.
Det. Div. Train.	(To be arranged by O.C., Div. Train.)					
One Battery 303 Bde. R.F.A.	Road junction just W. of BELLOY sur SOMME.	11.40 a.m.	BOURDON - HANGEST - CONDE.	"	2.27 p.m.	5.27 p.m.
Det. Div. Train.	(To be arranged by O.C., Div. Train.)					

APPENDIX. F

COPY No. 15

SECRET.

G/S.429.

A.D.C. for G.O.C.   Div. Train.
181 Inf. Bde.   D.S.C.
C.R.A.   A.D.V.S.
"A".   Camp Commandant.
A.D.M.S.   Fourth Army.
Signal Co.   XV Corps.
                           War Diary.

Units will entrain on the 22nd and 23rd November 1916 in accordance with attached Schedule "A" and Programmes of Entrainment.

Acknowledge.

H.Q., 60 Div.
20/11/16.

G. Bolton
Captain.
General Staff.

SECRET.   COPY No........

Ref. Map:LENS, Sheet 11. AMIENS, Sheet 17 &
ABBEVILLE, Sheet 14. 1/100,000.

PROGRAMME OF ENTRAINMENT.

22nd November 1916.

Troops.	Starting Point	Time of starting.	Route to station.	Entraining Station.	Time due at station.	Time of departure of train.
One Batty.,303 R.F.A.Bde.	Road Junction just W. of BELLOY sur SOMME	4.40.a.m.	BOURDON-HANGEST-CONDE.	LONGPRE.	7.27.a.m.	10.27.a.m.
Det.Div.Train.	(To be arranged by O.C., Div.Train).					
H.Q., 303 R.F.A. Bde.	Road junction just W. of BELLOY sur SOMME.	8.30.a.m.	BOURDON-HANGEST-CONDE.	"	11.17 a.m.	2.17.p.m.
303 R.F.A.Bde. Amm. Col.	"	"	"	"	"	"
One Batty.,303 R.F.A.Bde.	"	11.40.a.m.	"	"	2.27.p.m.	5.27.p.m.
Det.Div.Train.	(To be arranged by O.C., Div.Train).					

SECRET.

PROGRAMME OF ENTRAINMENT.

23rd November 1916.

COPY No. 15

Ref. Map: LENS, Sheet 11. AMIENS, Sheet 17.
ABBEVILLE, Sheet 14, .. 1/100,000.

Unit.	Starting Point.	Time of starting.	Route to entraining station.	Entraining station.	Time due at station.	Time of departure of train.
H.Q., 181 Inf.Bde.	Cross Roads, BRUCAMPS.	5.20.a.m.	VAUCHELLES les DOMART - LA FOLIE - L'ETOILE - CONDE.	LONGPRE.	7.27.a.m.	10.27.a.m.
2/23 Lond. R.	Cross Roads, ERGNIES.	5. 0.a.m.	AILLY-LONG-LE CATELET.	"	"	"
Y.60 & Z.60 T.M.Battys.	Cross Roads just W. of P of PONT REMY.	5.30.a.m.	LIERCOURT-FONTAINE.	"	"	"
One Batty. 303 R.F.A. Bde.	Road junction just W. of BELLOY sur SOMME.	8.30.a.m.	BOURDON-HANGEST-CONDE.	"	11.17.a.m.	2.17.p.m.
Det. Div. Train.	(To be arranged by O.C., Div. Train.)					
2/21 Lond. R.	Cross Roads, VILLERS-SOUS-AILLY.	12.40.p.m.	LONG-LE CATELET.	"	2.27.p.m.	5.27.p.m.
Det. Mob.Vet.Sec.	Cross Roads, AILLY LE HAUT CLOCHER.	12.30.p.m.	"	"	"	"

SECRET.

COPY No. 15

TABLE OF PERSONNEL, ANIMALS and VEHICLES
proceeding on the 22nd and 23rd November 1916.

SCHEDULE "A".

22nd November 1916.

No. of Train.	Type of Train.	Time of departure.	Unit.	Officers.	Other Ranks.	Animals.	Vehicles 4.W.	Vehicles 2.W.
26.	T.C.	10.27.a.m.	One Battery, 303 R.F.A.Bde. Det. Div. Train.	5. 4.	140. 100.	135. 49.	1. -	26. 13.
27.	T.C.	2.17.p.m.	H.Q., 303 R.F.A.Bde. 303 R.F.A.Bde.Amm.Col.	5. 3.	49. 198.	48. 136.	1. 2.	5. 34.
28.	T.C.	5.27.p.m.	One Battery, 303 R.F.A.Bde. Det. Div. Train.	5. 4.	140. 100.	135. 49.	1. -	26. 13.

23rd November 1916.

No. of Train.	Type of Train.	Time of departure.	Unit.	Officers.	Other Ranks.	Animals.	Vehicles 4.W.	Vehicles 2.W.
29.	Special x	10.27.a.m.	H.Q., 181 Inf.Bde. 2/23 Lond. R. Y.60 & Z.60 L..Bttys.	8. 39. 2.	40. 958. 46.	21. 84.	- -	- -
30.	T.C.	2.17.p.m.	One Btty.303 R.F.A.Bde. Det. Div. Train.	5. 4.	140. 100.	135. 49.	1 -	26. 13.
31.	Special ∅	5.27.p.m.	2/21 Lond. R. 60 Mob. Vet. Sec.	39.	958. 15.	84. 20.	-	-

Types of Trains. T.C. = Type Combatant, composed of .... 1st Class. Covered Trucks. Flat Trucks.
T.P. = Type Parc, composed of ....   1.   35.   12.
Special.* = Composed of..........   1.   24.   23.
* = Composed of..........   1.   27.
∅ = Composed of..........   2.   44.
                                                                    2.   42.

2 Brake Vans.

APPENDIX G

SECRET.   COPY NO. 15
                                                                  G/S. 431

A.D.C. for G.O.C.   Div. Train.
181 Inf. Bde.   D.S.C.
C.R.A.   A.D.V.S.
"A".   Camp Commandant.
A.D.M.S.   Fourth Army.
Signal Co.   XV Corps.
                               War Diary.
_____

   Units will entrain on the 24th November 1916 in
accordance with attached Schedule "A" and Programme of
Entrainment.

   Acknowledge.

                                        C.A.Bolton.
H.Q., 60th Division.   Captain.
21st November 1916.   General Staff.

SECRET.

COPY NO. 15
SCHEDULE "A".

TABLE OF PERSONNEL, ANIMALS and VEHICLES proceeding on the 24th November 1916.

No. of Train.	Type of Train.	Time of departure.	Unit.	Officers.	Other Ranks.	Animals.	Vehicles. 4 W.	Vehicles. 2 W.
32.	Special.	10.27 a.m.	2/22 Lond.R.	39.	958.	24.	-	-
			No. 4 Sec. Div.Sig.Co.	1.	27.	10.	-	-
33.	T.C.	2.17 p.m.	60 San. Sec.	1.	29.	9.	-	4.
			Div. H.Q.	7.	137.	77.	-	8.
			Det. 2/6 Fd. Amb.	2.	40.	25.	3.	-
			Det. Div. Train.	4.	200.	40.	-	12.
34.	Special.	5.27 p.m.	No. 1 S.A.A. Sec. Amm. Col.	3.	255.	25.	1.	-
			No. 3 S.A.A. Sec. Amm. Col.	3.	255.	25.	-	-
			Det. 2/6 Fd. Amb.	9.	369.	42.	-	-
			H.Q., Div. R.A.	2.	4.	-	-	-

	1st Class.	Covered Trucks.	Flat Trucks.
	1.	33.	14.
	1.	47.	-

Types of Trains. T.C. = Type Combatant, composed of ....
Special. = Composed of ....

SECRET.

COPY NO. 15.

PROGRAMME OF ENTRAINMENT.

Ref. Map: LENS, Sheet 11, ARRAS, Sheet 17. 24th November 1916.
ABBEVILLE, Sheet 14. 1/100,000.

Unit.	Starting Point.	Time of starting.	Route to entraining station.	Entraining Station.	Time due at Time of departure station. of train.
2/23 Lond.R.	Crossroads BRUCAMPS.	5.20 a.m.	VAUCHELLES-l-s-DOMART LA FOLIE – L'ETOILE – CONDE.	LONGPRE.	7.27 a.m. 10.27 a.m.
No. 4 Sec. Div. Sig. Co.	"	5.25 a.m.	"	"	" "
Div. H.Q.	Crossroads AILLY LE HAUT CLOCHER.	9.20 a.m.	LONG – LE CATELET.	"	11.17 a.m. 2.17 p.m.
60 San. S.C.	"	9.20 a.m.	"	"	" "
Det. 2/6 Fd. Amb.	La FOLIE Crossroads	10.15 a.m.	L'ETOILE – CONDE.	"	" "
Det. Div.Train. (To be arranged by O.C., Div. Train.)					
No. 1 S.A.A. Crossroads S.W. of Col. BETHENCOURT.		12 noon	FLIXECOURT – CONDE. BOURDON – HANGEST	"	2.27 p.m. 5.27 p.m.
No. 3 S.A.A. Road junction just N. of Col. BELLOY sur SOLE.		11.40 a.m.	CONDE.	"	" "
Det. 2/6 Fd. Amb.	LA FOLIE Crossroads.	1.0 p.m.	L'ETOILE – CONDE.	"	" "
H.Q., Div.R...	Road junction S. of AILLY LE HAUT CLOCHER.	12.40 p.m.	LONG – LE CATELET.	"	" "

APPENDIX 'H'

MOVE OF THE 60TH DIVISION.

PROGRAMME FOR NOVEMBER 25th 1916.

The Units detailed in Q.M.G's letter No.5885
dated 22.11.16 will entrain as follows:-

From LONGPRE.

	Depart.	Marche.	Off.	O.R.	Horses.	Motor Cycles.
35th Train (Special) 46 Covered Trucks and 2 Coaches.						
	10.27.	H.T.6.				
Battalion (½) 181st Inf Bde			21	479	10	-
Divisional Train.			8	520	60	-
36th Train (Special) 40 Covered Trucks and 2 Coaches.						
	14.17.	H.T.10.				
Field Company. 3/5			6	235	24	-
M.G.Company 181			10	172	10	-
Battalion (½) 181st Inf Bde			18	479	14	-
Divisional H.Q.			2	4	-	-
Div. Signals.			-	4	-	4

G.H.Q.

22nd November 1916

C.W.Hartopp
Lieut:
for D.D.R.T.(T).

A/1611/79

2 Copies to:- Q.M.G.
10 " " 60th Division.
2 " " A.D.R.T. IV.
6 " " D.A.D.R.T. MARSEILLES.
1 Copy to R.T.O. LONGPRE.
1 " " Base Commandant, MARSEILLES.

"G" for information.

Units will entrain according to
above programme on 25th inst arriving
at station three hours before train is
timed to leave. No further orders will
be issued.

J.E. Oswald Capt
for A.A.Q.M.G.
22-11-16   60th Divn

Army Form A 2007.

CENTRAL REGISTRY.

Central Registry No. and Date.

502/84 (G).

Attached Files.

SUBJECT, AND OFFICE OF ORIGIN.

Minor Operations - Raid.
Carried out by 2/15th London Regt. on night
15/11th September, 1916.

60th Div

Referred to	Date	Referred to	Date	Referred to	Date
G.	15.9.16				
I.	18.9.16				
Jrn MGRA	18.9.16				
CE	19.9.16				
G.	20.9.16				

3026

P.A.	Date

Schedule of Correspondence

Secret

H.Q. 17th Corps.

Forwarded.

I gathered from the units concerned that several Germans were killed in the trenches and much damage done.

11.9.16.

60th Division.

1st Army.

Forwarded. The raid appears to have been well planned and executed.

Charles Ferguson
Lt General
Comm. 17th Corps.

12.9.1916

To G.O.C. 179th Inf. Brigade.

Report on Raid.
10/11 September, 1916.

In accordance with raid Operation Orders already forwarded our raid on the German trenches was successfully carried out this morning at 3 a.m.

The party left our lines at 2-45 a.m. and were all back at 3-30 a.m.

Casualties.
2 Officers wounded
4 men   "   of whom one has since died.

Prisoners.
Four prisoners were taken of whom one was severely wounded.
All prisoners belonged to the 184th Regt. The unwounded prisoners were at once despatched to advance Brigade Head Quarters.

Conduct.

Officers.
I cannot speak too highly of the work performed by Lieut. Peatfield, and 2d Lieut. Thompson in organising and carrying out the raid. They had forgotten no detail, had the full confidence of their men and behaved throughout with coolness and gallantry. I hope that they may be considered for special recognition.

Conduct. O. R.
Non-commissioned officers and men all did well and showed great keenness both during training and in the actual operation. I hope that the following may be considered for reward or mention :-
    Corporal Jones
    Sergt. Quinton
    Corporal Marshall
    Pte. *names will be submitted later*
    Pte.

State of enemy *trenches etc*
As both officers are wounded it is not possible to obtain a good account of the German trenches, but it appears that at the point entered the trenches are very wide (12 ft. ?) and deep.
The morale of the enemy was low and the only opposition encountered was from bombing parties in two small trenches immediately E. of point of entry and which we had originally intended to include in our raid.

(1)

Artillery (a) Our own artillery fire was most accurate and effective and completely covered our withdrawal.

(b) The enemy's artillery was feeble and badly directed. They placed a barrage on the Elbe and Claudot trenches but caused no casualties.

Methods. All plans and methods for carrying out and facilitating the raid worked well and the two which were perhaps most useful were :
  (1) Paper chase trail
  (2) Decoy guiding lanterns

These latter were put up on posts 60 yards apart and about 500 yards N. of our point of re-entry to our own line. Much of the enemy artillery and Torpedo fire was directed on these lanterns.

Medical arrangements. Owing to lack of suitable dugout accommodation it was impossible to establish an aid post in front line, but a party of bearers were at the point of re-entry and no difficulty was experienced in dealing with casualties.

Subsequent. Since the return of our party several small parties of Germans have been noticed in no man's land evidently trying to find their missing men or to pick up the trail of our party. Two of the enemy approached one of our posts at about 4 a.m. and were unfortunately bombed instead of being shot by the men on duty.

Further details. Any further details which may be received will be forwarded in an additional report.

Officers' reports. I attach statements made to me by Lieuts. Peatfield and Thompson and there is no doubt that these statements can be amplified later.

Cooperation. The Co-operation of Trench Mortars and Stokes Guns and Machine Guns was most valuable, especially the latter, which enabled us to stop enemy wiring parties and protected our flanks on a part of the ground which the artillery could not deal with.

11/9/1916.

de Putron. Lt. Col.
Coy 7/15th Battn London Regt.

Statement by Lieut. B. PEATFIELD.

The night previous to the raid was quiet. A German working party of approximately five men had been heard from 10 p.m. to midnight at work on the wire. Lewis gun fire was brought to bear on this party but their work was continued inside the German trenches.

At 2-15 a.m. Lieutenant Peatfield and 2nd Lieut. Thompson carried out the impedimenta, ladders and blankets, etc., to the head of the sap at point of departure.

At 2-30 a.m. the men were lined up in the sap.

At 2-45 a.m. the head of the party left the sap and crawled out toward a point in the German line previously selected and noted by compass bearing, 150 degrees magnetic.

Although the moon was obscured by cloud, a sniper fired upon the party on leaving the sap and bombs were thrown from the North but no damage was done. The head of the party reached the cover of thistles about 15 yards from the German wire and there awaited our Artillery fire.

The first salvo was fired at 3 a.m. whereupon the party rose up and walked to the wire.

The German wire was damaged but not wholly cut and the ground about the wire was cut up by shell holes.

The wire was 12 to 15 yards in depth and was successfully crossed by blanket bridges.

The bombing party entered the trench and proceeded to block it in accordance with the previously arranged programme.

The centre party found a German dugout at point of entry. 2nd Lieut. Thompson threw a bomb down the dugout, wounding some of the occupants, who were ordered in German to come out, with a threat that further bombs would be thrown. They obeyed and prisoners were taken and escorted back to our lines.

The party was in the German trenches about ten minutes.

The morale of the prisoners was exceedingly low, and they were so terrified that it was only with great difficulty they could be induced to come out of their trench.

The party was recalled at point of entry by code word, and retired in good order, bringing one of our party, who was wounded and helpless.

Much time was lost in getting both German and our wounded out of the trenches, and again crossing the wire with the casualties on the return journey. When the whole party had successfully evacuated the German trench, I handed over command to 2nd Lieut. THompson as I felt weak from loss of blood, and feared I might have to be carried back.

In all four prisoners were taken, two of whom were I think wounded.

The Artillery fire was accurate and effective.

A further report from 2nd Lieut. Thompson will follow.

During the raid 2nd Lieut. Thompson acted with the greatest coolness and courage. The success of the raid in a great measure is due to his work.

The conduct of the men left nothing to be desired.

The Germans manned a little trench running South from point of entry immediately behind the main trench, and it was from this point that the bombs were thrown.

I laid a paper chase trail when going out which was extremely useful on the return journey.

11/9/1916.

Statement by 2nd Lieut. THOMPSON.

We went over and met with absolutely no opposition till we were in the German trench, except from one sniper.

We were absolutely unopposed going over, except for one man in the trench, who they got out at once.

Corporal Jones's party ran on then and went up and blocked the left sap, but I stuck to the dugout just were we entered the trench.

The next thing was I stood at the dugout door and ordered them to come out. I kept on shouting .... and I caught two of them coming out, whom I passed back to the man behind me, but whom it was I could not say, though I don't know about the dugout on the left.

The next thing was I sent to Mr Peatfield if we should send the word "retire".

As I got the word passed along I went to the bottom of the steps where I met the fellows and got them to report when all were in. They climbed up the ladders and got out.

The last party to come out was Corporal Jones's party, and two of them got left.

Corporal Jones came running back to me to say he had a badly wounded man, and I immediately went back and we shouted to some of the men to help him up the ladder.

We stood and bombed the trenches left and right while they were being got up. At any rate we got them up, and the man that was hit on the ladder. I got another man to help.

Both the covering party as well as the bombers were got back.

Nobody else was hit and we got together a little covering party.

Corporal Jones, Sergeant Quinton and Corporal Blick stayed behind, and it took them a considerable time to get them down to the sap. We held the sap head until I got the word passed up that the final party had got into the dugout.

Then I called in the covering party and got them into the Paris Redoubt and got them all down into the dugout somehow, after which I crawled down myself. It was some time before I could make sure that everybody was in.

11/9/1916.

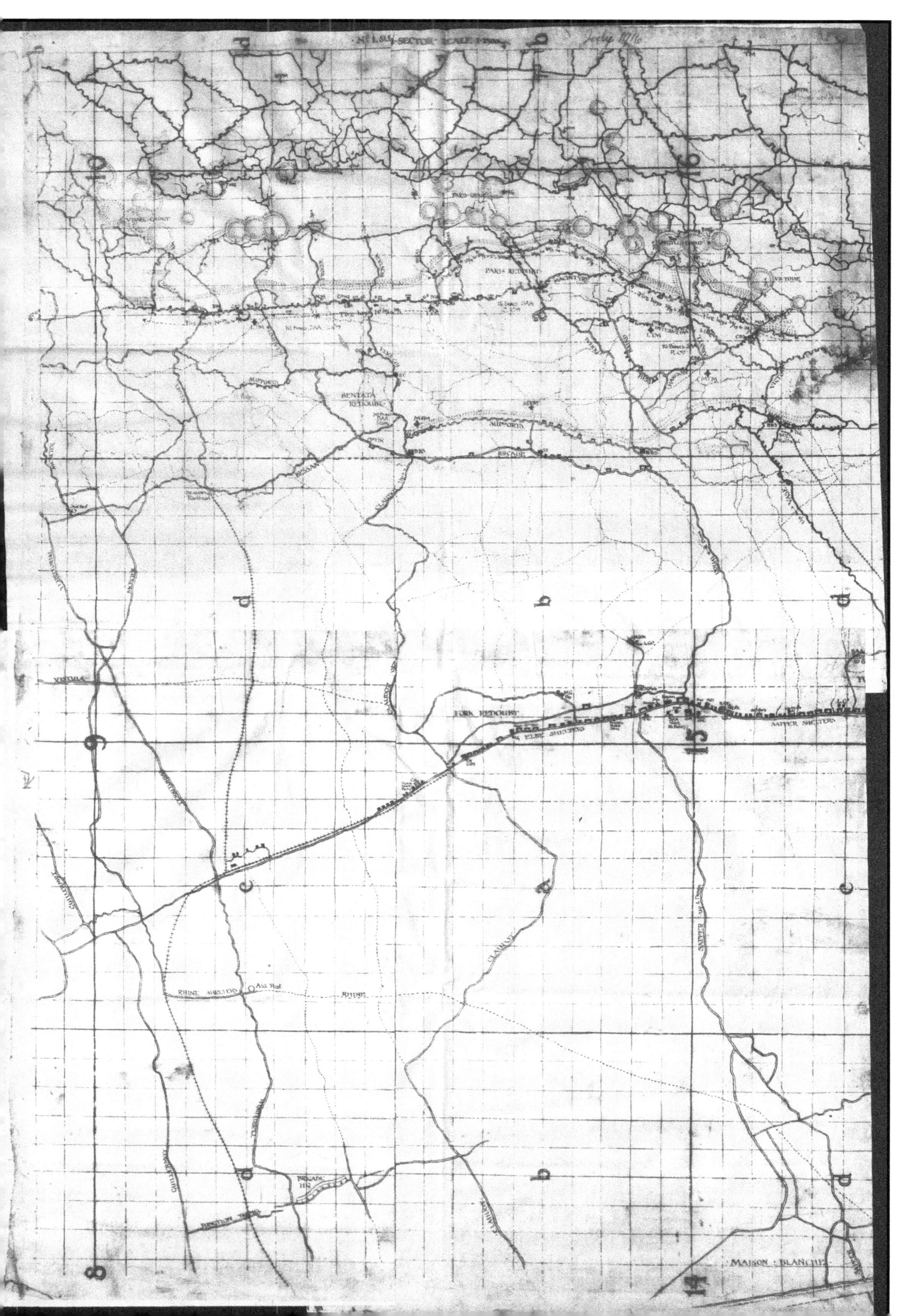

60th Division No. G.S.288.

H.Q.
XVII Corps.

Forwarded.

I gathered from the units concerned that several Germans were killed in the trenches and much damage done.

(Sgd) E.S.Bulfin.
Major-General.
Commanding 60th (London) Division.

11/9/16.

(2)

First Army.

Forwarded.

The raid appears to have been well planned and executed.

(Sgd) Charles Fergusson.
Lieut-General.
Commanding XVII Corps.

12/9/16.

To G.O.C. 179th Infantry Brigade.

REPORT ON RAID.
10th/11th September, 1916.

In accordance with raid Operation Orders already forwarded our raid on the German trenches was successfully carried out this morning at 3 a.m.

The party left our lines at 2.45 a.m. and were all back at 3.30 a.m.

<u>Casualties</u>. 2 officers wounded.
4 men wounded, of whom one has since died.

<u>Prisoners</u>. Four prisoners were taken of whom one was severely wounded.

All prisoners belonged to the 184th Regt. The unwounded prisoners were at once despatched to advance brigade headquarters.

<u>Conduct</u>.
<u>Officers</u>. I cannot speak too highly of the work performed by Lieut. PEATFIELD and 2nd/Lieut. THOMPSON in organising and carrying out the raid. They had forgotten no detail had the full confidence of their men and behaved throughout with coolness and gallantry. I hope that they may be considered for special recognition.

<u>Conduct</u>.
<u>Men</u>. Non-commissioned officers and men all did well and showed great keenness both during training and in the actual operation. I hope that the following may be considered for reward or mention :-

   Corporal JONES.
   Sergt. QUINTON.
   Corporal MARSHALL.
   Pte.)
   Pte.) Names will be submitted later.

<u>State of trenches etc</u>. As both officers are wounded it is not possible to obtain a good account of the German trenches, but

(2)

it appears that at the point entered the trenches are very wide (12 feet. ?) and deep.

The morale of the enemy was low and the only opposition encountered was from bombing parties in two small trenches immediately E. of point of entry and which we had originally intended to include in our raid.

Artillery. (a) Our own artillery fire was most accurate and effective and completely covered our withdrawal.

(b) The enemy's artillery was feeble and badly directed. They placed a barrage on the ELBE and CLAUDOT trenches but caused no casualties.

Methods. All plans and methods for carrying out and facilitating the raid worked well and the two which were perhaps most useful were :-
(1) Paper chase trail.
(2) Decoy guiding lanterns.

These latter were put up on posts 60 yards apart and about 500 yards N. of our point of re-entry to our own line. Much of the enemy artillery and torpedo fire was directed on these lanterns.

Medical arrangements. Owing to lack of suitable dugout accommodation it was impossible to establish an aid post in front line, but a party of bearers were at the point of re-entry and no difficulty was experienced in dealing with casualties.

Subsequent. Since the return of our party several small parties of Germans have been noticed in No man's Land evidently trying to find their missing men or to pick up the trail of our party. Two of the enemy approached one of our posts at about 4 a.m. and were unfortunately bombed instead of being shot by the men on duty.

Further Details.   Any further details which may be
    received will be forwarded in an additional report.

Officers' Reports.   I attach statements made to me by Lieuts.
    PEATFIELD and THOMPSON and there is no doubt that these
    statements can be amplified later.

Co-operation.   The co-operation of trench mortars and Stokes
    guns and machine guns was most valuable, especially
    the latter, which enabled us to stop enemy wiring parties
    and protected our flanks on a part of the ground which
    the artillery could not deal with.

                                (Sgd) C.de Putron.
                                        Lieut-Colonel.
11/9/16.   Commanding 2/15th Battn. London Regt.

STATEMENT BY LIEUT. B. PEATFIELD.

The night previous to the raid was quiet. A German working party of approximately five men had been heard from 10 p.m. to midnight at work on the wire. Lewis gun fire was brought to bear on this party but their work was continued inside the German trenches.

At 2.15 a.m. Lieutenant PEATFIELD and 2nd/Lieut. THOMPSON carried out the impedimenta, ladders and blankets, etc. to the head of the sap at point of departure.

At 2.30 a.m. the men were lined up in the sap.

At 2.45 a.m. the head of the party left the sap and crawled out toward a point in the German line previously selected and noted by compass bearing, 150 degrees magnetic.

Although the moon was obscured by cloud, a sniper fired upon the party on leaving the sap and bombs were thrown from the North but no damage was done. The head of the party reached the cover of thistles about 15 yards from the German wire and there awaited our artillery fire.

The first salvo was fired at 3 a.m. whereupon the party rose up and walked to the wire.

The German wire was damaged but not wholly cut and the ground about the wire was cut up by shell holes.

The wire was 10 to 15 yards in depth and was successfully crossed by blanket bridges.

The bombing party entered the trench and proceeded to block it in accordance with the previously arranged programme.

The centre party found a German dugout at point of entry. 2nd/Lieut. THOMPSON threw a bomb down the dugout, wounding some of the occupants, who were ordered in German to come out, with a threat that further bombs would be thrown. They obeyed and prisoners were taken and escorted back to our lines.

The party was in the German trenches about ten minutes.

The morale of the prisoners was exceedingly low, and they were so terrified that it was only with great difficulty they could be indu induced to come out of their trench.

The party was recalled at point of entry by code word, and retired in good order, bringing one of our party, who was wounded and helpless.

Much time was lost in getting both German and our wounded out of the trenches, and again crossing the wire with the casualties on the return journey. When the whole party had successfully evacuated the German trench, I handed over command to 2nd/Lieut. THOMPSON as I felt weak from loss of blood, and feared I might have to be carried back.

In all four prisoners were taken, two of whom were I think wounded.

The artillery fire was accurate and effective.

A further report from 2nd/Lieut. THOMPSON will follow.

During the raid 2nd/Lieut. THOMPSON acted with the greatest coolness and courage. The success of the raid in a great measure is due to his work.

The conduct of the men left nothing to be desired.

The Germans manned a little trench running south from point of entry immediately behind the main trench, and it was from this point that the bombs were thrown.

I laid a paper chase trail when going out which was extremely useful on the return journey.

11/9/16.

STATEMENT BY 2ND/LIEUT. THOMPSON.

We went over and met with absolutely no opposition till we were in the German trench, except from one sniper.

We were absolutely unopposed going over, except for one man in the trench, who they got out at once.

Corporal Jones' party ran on then and went up and blocked the left sap, but I stuck to the dugout just where we entered the trench.

The next thing was I stood at the dugout door and ordered them to come out. I kept on shouting .... and I caught two of them coming out, whom I passed back to the man behind me, but whom it was I could not say, though I don't know about the dugout on the left.

The next thing was I sent to Mr. WEATFIELD if we should send the word "retire".

As I got the word passed along I went to the bottom of the steps where I met the fellows and got them to report when all were in. They climbed up the ladders and got out.

The last party to come out was Corporal JONES's party, and two of them got left.

Corporal JONES came running back to me to say he had a badly wounded man, and I immediately went back and we shouted to some of the men to help him up the ladder.

We stood and bombed the trenches left and right while they were being got up. At any rate we got them up, and the man that was hit on the ladder. I got another man to help.

Both the covering party was as well as the bombers were got back.

Nobody else was hit and we got together a little covering party.

Corporal JONES, Sergeant QUINTON and Corporal BLICK stayed behind, and it took them a considerable time to get them down to the sap. We held the sap head until I got the word passed up that the final party had got into the dugout.

Then I called in the covering party and got them into the PARIS REDOUBT and got them all down into the dugout somehow, after which I crawled down myself. It was some time before I could make sure that everybody was in.

11/9/1916.

Army Form A 2007.

CENTRAL REGISTRY.

Central Registry No. and Date.

502/85 (G).

Attached Files.

SUBJECT, AND OFFICE OF ORIGIN.

Minor Operations - Raid
Carried out by 2/20th London Regt. on night
10th/11th September 1916.

60th Div

Referred to	Date	Referred to	Date	Referred to	Date
G.	15.9.16				
I	18.9.16				
J.10 MGRA	18.9.16				
CE	19.9.16				
G	20.9.16				

P.A.	Date

Schedule of Correspondence

Secret.
S.G.
17ᵗʰ Corps. 15.9.16   No. 502/85 (a).

Forwarded
Talking to the officers engaged in the raid I was informed that some six
Germans were killed and two dugouts set on fire. E.S. Bulfin Mjr.
11.9.16.
                                    60ᵗʰ Division.

2

1ˢᵗ Army.

   Forwarded. This raid was successful
in securing a good identification. It was
a difficult place to take on, and
credit is due to all concerned. It seems
probable that 2 prisoners broke away
the while being brought in, and were
pursued by the three men missing —

                        Charles Fergusson
                              Lt General
12.9.1916   Comm. 17ᵗʰ Corps.

Report on Raid carried out by C/20th Battn.London
Regiment on night of 10/11th September 1916.

Weather. Fine, Light, Slightly Misty.

No Mans Land. Ropes had previously been laid across this; every man of the party had been across at least once before by his particular route. During the last two nights excellent work had been done by 2nd.Lieut. L.E.M.Weatherley watching the wire; acting on his information, our Lewis Gunners had stopped several enemy wiring parties.
In fact, the raiding party found material laying on parapet all ready for the wiring party.

Enemy Wire. This had been most excellently cut by 2nd.Lieut. Sharp (Trench Mortar Battery) during the last three days, who acted in close co-operation with 2nd.Lieut. Weatherley and his patrols.

Trenches. 8' deep, nearly twice as wide as ours. Fire steps in places 3' wide, revetted with hurdles and planks. Duckboard floors. Trenches were very bare and in good condition, except for very bad damage probably done by our 9" Mortar.

Dug-outs. One in nearly every firebay. All in parapet, depth about 15 feet, only connected in some cases: chambers small, most only had one entrance. Some very badly knocked about, and empty. In two firebays at least the flooring was concrete.

Action of 3 Parties.

(1) 2nd.Lieut.Thompson's party.

Corpl.Painter knocked down and captured a German directly they reached the Sap. 2nd.Lieut.Thompson found, and went down three dug-outs which were all empty. These dug outs and the trench were much knocked about and difficult to get along. Also our T.M.Shells were dropping very near.

(2) Lieut.Crafter's party

Lieut. Crafter went down a deep dug out and found two Red Cross men in it, whom he took prisoners. The next dug out had two Infantrymen in it - both were given to the booty party, one man, but was shot, and fell and remained in the barbed wire. Lieut.Crafter went into two more "dug-outs" which were empty.

(3) 2nd.Lieut. Woolfe's party, found about 6 men in the trench, of whom two were killed, and the rest ran away northwards up the trench.
2nd.Lieut.Woolfe found two "dug-outs" in two adjoining fire bays - he fired a revolver shot down each, and called upon the inmates to come out. Two came out of the second one.
He could still hear talking, and was fired at from the bottom of the "dug-out", but no more Bosche would come out, so he threw down a Mills and a "P" Bomb into each dug-out.

Prisoners.	Four prisoners were brought in belonging to the 122nd.Regt, of whom one was a Red Cross N.C.O., and another a Red Cross Private. It is not clear why six prisoners were taken and only four brought back; evidence points to the explanation being that two were shot on the way back; the fact that three of our men are missing, but were seen returning over the German parapet may corroborate this. There is pretty certain evidence that five Germans were killed in the enemy trenches.
Return.	2nd.Lieut. Woolfe's party returned early, as he had broken his watch. Lieut. Crafter followed shortly. 2nd.Lieut.Thompson got back at 3.55 a.m.

Booty	A complete kit of a German Red Cross "Unter Officizier" was brought back which included a short bayonet, and an automatic pistol.
	    Another N.C.O's cap and a Very Pistol were captured, which points to another N.C.O having escaped.
	    A complete list of booty is attached.

Gas	There appeared to be no protection against Gas, and no telephone wires were seen.
Our Casualties	Two men wounded Three men missing at 3.15 a.m.
Barrage	was accurate and effective.
Hostile Enemy Fire.	Artillery very slight. A certain amount of rifle fire, Machine Gun, and Rifle Grenades.
Communication.	Special telephone lines had been laid and worked well, as is shown in attached list of messages.

The whole raid had been carefully organised and re-hearsed by Capt & Adjt W.M.Craddock, to whose great care and organising power, more than anything else, I attribute the success of the raid.
    The execution was well carried out by the three Officers, and other members of the raiding party, particularly good work being done by Corporal Painter and Private Castel (who acted as interpreter to Lieut. Crafter).

Lt.Crafter.
2/Lt.Thompson
2/Lt.Woolfe.

11.9.16.

W.S.H.Warde-Aldam
Lt.Col.
Comdg. 2/20 th Bn. London Regt.

H.Q. 60th Division

Forwarded. I think this all went very well

H.W.Shedd B.General

LIST OF BOOTY.

1 Set of Equipment, Infantry.

1 Entrenching Tool.

1 Cap.

1 Rifle 1916.

1 Very Pistol.

2 Bags containing, Rations and Kit.

1 Set Equipment of a Medical N.C.O.

W.R. Warde-Aldam
Lt. Colonel,
Condg., 2/20th. Battn. London Regt.

11-9-16.

3.10 a.m.   First Man Over.

3.25 a.m.   Everything quiet, no opposition.

3.26 a.m.   First Very Lights sent up.

3.27 a.m.   Some Sniping and Rifle Grenades.

3.28 a.m.   First Machine Gun.

3.30 a.m.   First shell from Barrage.

3.35 a.m.   3 or 4 prisoners on the way.

3.37 a.m.   Everything going well.

3.40 a.m.   One more just come in.
               Most of them back.
               One casualty, slight, reported.

3.45 a.m.   Crafter's and Woolfe's parties returned.

3.49 a.m.   Think all in, waiting Partridge's check.

3.55 a.m.   Check still going on.

4.20 a.m.   Feel sure all in, but three men not reported
               yet to Partridge. Are any of them at
               Headquarters?

5.5. a.m.   Have sent search party out for three men not
               reported.

5.30 a.m.   Search party returned, no news of men not
               reported.

6.15 a.m.   Closed station.

S E C R E T.   60th Division. No G.S.287.

H.Q.
   XVII Corps.

      Forwarded.
      Talking to the officers engaged in the raid, I was informed that some six Germans were killed and two dug-outs set on fire.

                                         (sgd). E. S. BULFIN, M.G.

11-9-16.   60th Division.

                              - 2 -

1st Army.

      Forwarded.
      This raid was successful in securing a good identification. It was a difficult place to take on, and credit is due to all concerned. It seems probable that two prisoners broke away while being brought in, and were pursued by the three men missing.

                                         (sgd). CHARLES FERGUSSON,

12-9-16.   Lieutenant-General,
                                                Commanding XVII Corps.

REPORT on RAID carried out by 2/20th Battn.
London Regiment, on night of 10th/11th
September 1916.

Weather.   Fine, light, slightly misty.

NO MAN'S LAND.   Ropes had previously been laid across this; every man of
                 the party had been across at least once before by his
                 particular route. During the last two nights excellent
                 work had been done by 2nd/Lieut. L. E. M. WEATHERLEY
                 watching the wire; acting on his information our Lewis
                 gunners had stopped several enemy wiring parties. In
                 fact, the raiding party found material laying on parapet
                 ready for the wiring party.

Enemy wire.   This had been most excellently cut by 2nd/Lieut. SHARP
                 (Trench Mortar Battery) during the last three days, who
                 acted in close co-operation with 2nd/Lieut. WEATHERLEY
                 and his patrols.

Trenches.   8' deep, nearly twice as wide as ours. Fire steps in
                 places nearly 3' wide, revetted with hurdles and planks.
                 Duckboard floors. Trenches were very bare and in good
                 condition, except for very bad damage probably done by our
                 2" mortar.

Dug-outs.   One in nearly every firebay. All in parapet, depth about
                 15 feet, only connected in some cases; chambers small,
                 most only had one entrance. Some very badly knocked about
                 and empty. In two firebays at least the flooring was
                 concrete.

Action of   (1) 2nd/Lieut. THOMPSON'S party.
3 Parties.
                      Corpl. PAINTER knocked down and captured a German
                 directly they reached the sap. 2nd/Lieut. THOMPSON
                 found, and went down, three dug-outs which were all
                 empty. These dug-outs and the trench were much
                 knocked about and difficult to get along. Also our
                 T.M. shells were dropping very near.

                 (2) Lieut. CRAFTER'S party.

                      Lieut. CRAFTER went down a deep dugout and found
                 two Red Cross men in it, whom he took prisoners. The
                 next dug-out had two infantrymen in it - both were
                 given to the booty party; one ran, but was shot, and
                 fell and remained in the barbed wire. Lieut. CRAFTER
                 went into two more dug-outs, which were empty.

                 (3) 2nd/Lieut. WOOLFE'S party.

                      Found about 6 men in the trench, of whom 2 were
                 killed, and the rest ran away northwards up the trench.
                 2nd/Lieut. WOOLFE found two dug-outs in two adjoining
                 firebays - he fired a revolver shot down each and
                 called upon the inmates to come out. Two came out of
                 the second one. He could still hear talking and was
                 fired at from the bottom of the dug-out, but no more
                 Bosches would come out, so he threw down a Mills and
                 a "P" bomb into each dug-out.

- 2 -

Prisoners.	Four prisoners were brought in belonging to the 122nd Regt, of whom one was a Red Cross N.C.O., and another a Red Cross private. It is not clear why six prisoners were taken and only four brought back; evidence points to the explanation being that two were shot on the way back; the fact that three of our men are missing, but were seen returning over the German parapet, may corroborate this. There is pretty certain evidence that five Germans were killed in the enemy trenches.
Return.	2nd/Lieut. WOOLFE'S party returned early, as he had broken his watch. Lieut. CRAFTER followed shortly after. 2nd/Lieut. THOMPSON got back at 3.55 a.m.
Booty.	A complete kit of a German Red Cross "unter officizier" was brought back which included a short bayonet and an automatic pistol. Another N.C.O's cap and a Very pistol were captured, which points to another N.C.O. having escaped. A complete list of booty is attached.
Gas.	There appears to be no protection against gas, and no telephone wires were seen.
Our casualties.	Two men wounded - three men missing at 8.15 a.m.
Barrage.	Was accurate and effective.
Hostile enemy fire.	Artillery very slight. A certain amount of rifle fire, machine gun and rifle grenades.
Communication.	Special telephone lines had been laid and worked well, as is shown in attached list of messages.
Lt.Crafter. 2/Lt.Thompson. 2/Lt.Woolfe.	The whole raid had been carefully organised and rehearsed by Capt. and Adjt. W. N. CRADDOCK, to whose great care and organising power, more than anything else, I attribute the success of the raid. The execution was well carried out by the three officers and other members of the raiding party, particularly good work being done by Corporal PAINTER and Private CASTEL (who acted as interpreter to Lieut. CRAFTER).

(sgd). W. S. A. WARDE-ALDAM,
Lt.Col.

11. 9. 16.   Comdg. 2/20th Battn.London Rgt

H.Q. 60th Division.

Forwarded. I think that all went very well.

H. W. STUDD,
Br.General.

LIST of BOOTY.

1 set of Equipment, Infantry.
1 Entrenching Tool.
1 Cap.
1 Rifle, 1916.
1 Very Pistol.
2 bags containing Rations and Kit.
1 set Equipment of a Medical N.C.O.

                        (sgd). W.S.A. WARDE-ALDAM

                                      Lt.Col.
11-9-16.   Cmdg. 2/20th Battn, London Regt.

                        (sgd). H.W. STUDD,
                                Br.General.

LIST of MESSAGES.

3.10 a.m.	First man over.
3.25 a.m.	Everything quiet, no opposition.
3.26 a.m.	First Very lights sent up.
3.27 a.m.	Some sniping and rifle grenades.
3.28 a.m.	First machine gun.
3.30 a.m.	First shell from barrage.
3.35 a.m.	3 or 4 prisoners on the way.
3.37 a.m.	Everything going well.
3.40 a.m.	One more just come in. Most of them back. One casualty, slight, reported. 3.45. CRAFTER'S and WOOLFE'S partys returned.
3.49 a.m.	Think all in, waiting PARTRIDGE'S check.
3.55 a.m.	Check still going on.
4.20 a.m.	Feel sure all in, but three men are not reported yet to PARTRIDGE. Are any of them at headquarters?
5.5. a.m.	Have sent search party out for 3 men not reported.
5.50 a.m.	Search party returned, no news of men not reported.
6.15 a.m.	Closed station.

                                  (sgd). H.W. STUDD
                                        Br.General.

Army Form A. 2007.

CENTRAL REGISTRY.

Central Registry No. and Date.

502/104(G)

Attached Files.

SUBJECT, AND OFFICE OF ORIGIN.

Minor Operations — Raid
Carried out by 2/17th London Regt against
enemy trenches in S.28.A. West of LA FOLIE FARM.
on morning of 9th October.
60th Div

Referred to	Date	Referred to	Date	Referred to	Date
Jm	G. 12.10.16				
	I. 11.10.16	used			
	AERO 11.10.16				
	CE 11.10.16				
	G. 23.10.16				

P. A. | Date

Schedule of Correspondence.

21

First Army No. 502/104(G)

XVII Corps

Reference your G.698, d/- 12/10/16

The Army Commander considers the raid carried out by the 60th Division on the 9th October to have been well planned and well executed.

(sd) G. d. S. Barrow

16th October 1916.

Major-General,
General Staff, First Army.

SECRET

General Staff, XVII Corps. No. 4698

1st Army.   502/104(k)
                13/10/16
Forwarded. This raid was well planned and executed, and the efficiency of the communications was particularly satisfactory.

Charles Fergusson
Lt. Genl.
12.10.1916   Comm. XVII Corps

SECRET

To Headquarters,
   60th (London) Division.

The raid on the enemy's trenches carried out by a party of the 2/17th Battalion, London Regt. under the Command of Lieut. F.O.Woodman, at 1.50.a.m. on 9th October 1916, was completely successful in achieving the results which it was desired to attain.

Every detail had been carefully thought out and each member of the party knew what was expected of him, and carried out his job thoroughly.

When the enemy would not come out of his dug-outs, Lieut. Woodman and the other two Officers went down the dug-outs or mine shafts to fetch them out.

The whole operation was executed, not only with great gallantry, but in a thoroughly practical and business like way, and resulted in 6 prisoners being brought back to our lines, and 6 or 7 of the enemy being killed.

The work being completed the return signal was given, 11 minutes after Zero.

I attach a list of the telephone messages, which were sent to Brigade Headquarters during the raid.

The completeness and promptitude with which I was informed of all that passed, are an additional indication of the well thought out and thorough nature of the organization, which characterized the whole of the operation as planned and carried out by Lieut.Colonel Houlder, and Lieut.Woodman to whom, and to all ranks who took part in the raid great praise is due.

BRIGADIER-GENERAL.
Commanding 180th Infantry Brigade.

ADV. BRIGADE H.Q.
11th October 1916.

Report by O.C. 2/17 London Regt. is attached.

Headquarters
17th Corps.

Forwarded —
Next-better raid after 19th Battn, also in this Brigade, I regard this raid as the second best undertaken by the Division.

From Officer Commanding,
         2/17th Battalion, London Regt.

To G.O.C. 180th Infantry Brigade.

                    Raiding Operations night of 8/9th Oct.1916.

Sir,
        I have the honour to report that in accordance with the orders which were submitted to you, a Raid was carried out under the Command of Lieut. F.O.Woodman at 1.50.am. 9th Oct.1916.

        The party left the British Lines at 1.48.a.m. crossed No Man's Land and arrived opposite the German lines at about 1.50.a.m. The Artillery as arranged at this time carried out their barrage which was assisted by a barrage from the 2" Trench Mortars and Stokes Guns.

        The parties entered the trench at the point arranged Lieut.F.L.White's party entered the trench and proceeded to-wards the right, they discovered one German in a shelter, who after some resistance surrendered and was sent back to the British Lines under escort at once. Lieut.White proceeded some ten yards beyond the shelter to the entrance of what proved to be a mine shaft, he entered this himself and was joined by Lieut. Woodman, in the meantime his party where proceeding further to the right up the trench, searching for Germans and with the object of discovering another entrance to the shaft.

        Lieut.White and Lieut.Woodman entered the mine shaft and proceeded down the steps some twenty feet underground where they found a small chamber leading to the left, this had a bed and tarpaulin in it, but there were no other signs of occupation. They came out of this chamber and descended another thirty feet from whence they could see the bottom of the shaft and white chalk passages running up either way. They noticed metal covered hose pipe reaching from the top of the shaft to the bottom, and as they heard no sound of any one at the bottom of the shaft, they returned to the top.

        Before meeting Lieut.White, Lieut.Woodman had on entering the trench, pursued two Germans to the right, down the trench. The Germans fled up the Communication Trench, one of them being shot and killed by Lieut.Woodman.

        Lieut.Woodman and his party then discovered one dug-out smashed in by British fire, and searching along further, discovered another dug-out with two Germans in it, who surrendered at once, being in a great state of fear. Lieut. Woodman sent back the German prisoners and entered the mine shaft as stated above, with Lieut.White.

        Lieut.Woodman and Lieut.White got into the trenches after leaving the mine shaft, where they found a party of British carrying a wounded Bosche who was struggling violently with this party. As it had been ascertained that six prisoners had been captured unwounded, and as it was three minutes to the signal for recall, Lieut.Woodman gave the return signal on the French Horn and attempted to get the wounded Bosche over the top into No Man's Land the wounded German struggled violently and resisted, and eventually had to be shot.

                                        Lieut.Woodman

Lieut. Woodman and Lieut. White returned with their parties to the British Lines.

In the meantime Lieut. Goble had on entering the trenches at the appointed please turned to the left and at the head of his party proceeded down the trench towards point B. On passing through a bend in the trench near to where he entered Lieut. Goble saw three Germans running away down the trench. At the head of his men he pursued them, whereupon one of the Germans turned round and threw up his hands pleading for mercy. This man was taken prisoner and sent back, but in the meantime the two other Germans had managed to escape further up the trench and were pursued up to the entrance of a mine shaft. Lieut. Goble entered the shaft, but when approaching a chamber leading off to the right, (similar to the one already spoken of) was fired on by at least three Germans with their rifles, he called to the to surrender, in German, but they took no notice, and proceed to fire at the party with rifles and threw bombs ; whereupon the party replied with bombs and rifle fire, and prepared to rush the dug-out. At that time the signal for recall was heard from the top and Lieut. Goble after throwing all available bombs at the Germans, re-entered the trench, crossed No Man's Land, and returned to the British Trenches. The mine shaft appeared to be exactly similar to that described by Lieut. Woodman, in particular it had a similar steel covered piping.

The whole of the parties returned and were counted into the British trench. The Germans made no Artillery Retaliation whatever, but fired 3 rounds from Trench Mortars on "B" Company's lines by the SUNKEN ROAD.

The prisoners were taken to the Headquarters of "D" Coy, thence the Battalion Headquarters, and eventually to Brigade Headquarters.

Communication was established from point W, and information was collected there by Lieut. S.P. Davies, being passed down by telephone to "D" Coys Headquarters and thence to Battalion Headquarters.

The control of the Battalion front line trenches opposite the raided trench was under the direction of Lieut. R.G. Strutt.

The Regimental Aid Post was established at P.73 under the direction of the Medical Officer.

The recall signals (2 Bouquets of 6 red Rockets)* were fired from the vicinity of D Company's Headquarters, and guiding very lights were sent up from BEYLONES.

I have the honour to be

Sir

Your obedient servant.

(SGD.). C.F.G. HOULDER.

Lieut. Colonel.
Commanding 2/17th Battalion, London Rgt.

10th October 1916.

* Very lights were used, no rockets were fired.

TELEPHONE MESSAGES RECEIVED DURING THE RAID

of

2/17th London Regt.

1.50.a.m.	First Shot fired.
1.55.a.m.	Party start to time and is now in Bosche Line. (3 mins. to get through on phone.).
1.57.a.m.	Bombing in Bosche Line.
1.58.a.m.	Bringing three Bosch over. Another Bosche. (Making four). No retaliation. NO Bombing in Bosch trench. Four Bosche up to time. More returning (referring to raid party)
2.a.m.	More men returning. A whole crowd returning.
2.1.a.m.	The horn for returning is sounding, whole party coming back.
2.5.a.m.	No.retaliation. Party has reached our line, the party is being counted.
2.6.a.m.	Whole party returned safely. Hostile trench mortars open on "B" Coy.
2.7.a.m.	Regiment 104.
2.8.a.m.	Six Bosche Prisoners in all.
2.12.a.m. (Sting	Our Artillery have finished. No casualties reported yet. Artillery have ceased
(message. 2.15.a.m.	fire, but are standing by our targets. Everything quiet.
2.16.a.m.	The enemy have evidently returned behind DEVON.
2.25.a.m.	They think they killed four or five, full information not yet in.
2.40.a.m.	Bosche passing Battalion H.Q. on way down.
2.42.a.m.	Three wounded, very slightly, but will not require to leave the trenches.

SECRET

First Army.

GENERAL STAFF,
XVII CORPS.
No. 4698
Date.

Forwarded. This raid was well planned and executed, and the efficiency of the communications was particularly satisfactory.

(Sgd) CHARLES FERGUSSON.
Lieutenant-General.
Commanding XVII Corps.

12/10/1916.

SECRET.
                                                      60th Division No. G.S.374.
                                                      180th Inf.Bde. No.G.5102.

To Headquarters.
    60th (London) Division.

        The raid on the enemy's trenches carried out by a party of the 2/17th Battalion, London Regt. under the Command of Lieut. F.C.WOODMAN, at 1.50 a.m. on 9th October, 1916, was completely successful in achieving the results which it was desired to attain.

        Every detail had been carefully thought out and each member of the party knew what was expected of him, and carried out his job thoroughly.

        When the enemy would not come out of his dugouts, Lieut. WOODMAN and the other two officers went down the dugouts or mine shafts to fetch them out.

        The whole operation was executed, not only with great gallantry, but in a thoroughly practical and business-like way, and resulted in 6 prisoners being brought back to our lines, and 6 or 7 of the enemy being killed.

        The work being completed the return signal was given, 11 minutes after Zero.

        I attach a list of the telephone messages, which were sent to Brigade Headquarters during the raid.

        The completeness and promptitude with which I was informed of all that passed, are an additional indication of the well thought out and thorough nature of the organization which characterized the whole of the operation as planned and carried out by Lieut.Colonel HOULDER, and Lieut.WOODMAN to whom, and to all ranks who took part in the raid, great praise is due.

                                                      (Sgd) H.W.STUDD.
Adv.Brigade, H.Q.   Brigadier-General.
11th October, 1916.   Commanding 180th Infantry Brigade.

                                (2)

Headquarters.
    XVII Corps.

        Forwarded.
        Next to the raid of the 19th Battalion, also in this Brigade, I regard this raid as the second best undertaken by the division.

                                                  (Sgd) E.S.BULFIN.
                                                        Major-General.
11/10/16.   Commanding 60th (London) Division.

From Officer Commanding,
    2/17th Battalion, London Regt.

To G.O.C. 180th Infantry Brigade.

                Raiding Operations night 9th/10th October, 1916.

Sir,
       I have the honour to report that in accordance with the orders which were submitted to you, a raid was carried out under the command of Lieut. F.C.WOODMAN at 1.50 am. 9th Oct.1916.

       The party left the British lines at 1.45 a.m. crossed No Man's Land and arrived opposite the German lines at about 1.50 a.m. The artillery as arranged at this time carried out their barrage which was assisted by a barrage from the 2" trench mortars and Stokes guns.

       The parties entered the trench at the point arranged. Lieut. F.L.WHITE's party entered the trench and proceeded towards the right, they discovered one German in a shelter, who after some resistance surrendered and was sent back to the British lines under escort at once. Lieut. WHITE proceeded some ten yards beyond the shelter to the entrance of what proved to be a mine shaft, he entered this himself and was joined by Lieut.WOODMAN, in the meantime his party were proceeding further to the right up the trench, searching for Germans and with the object of discovering another entrance to the shaft.

       Lieut.WHITE and Lieut.WOODMAN entered the mine shaft and proceeded down the steps some twenty feet underground where they found a small chamber leading to the left, this had a bed and tarpaulin in it, but there were no other signs of occupation. They came out of this chamber and descended another thirty feet from whence they could see the bottom of the shaft and white chalk passages running up either way. They noticed metal covered hose pipe reaching from the top of the shaft to the bottom, and as they heard no sound of any one at the bottom of the shaft, they returned to the top.

       Before meeting Lieut.WHITE, Lieut.WOODMAN had on entering the trench, pursued two Germans to the right, down the trench. The Germans fled up the communication trench, one of them being shot and killed by Lieut.WOODMAN.

       Lieut.WOODMAN and his party then discovered one dugout smashed in by British fire, and searching along further, discovered another dugout with two Germans in it, who surrendered at once, being in a great state of fear. Lieut.WOODMAN sent back the German prisoners and entered the mine shaft as stated above, with Lieut. WHITE.

       Lieut.WOODMAN and Lieut.WHITE got into the trenches after leaving the mine shaft, where they found a party of British carrying a wounded Boche who was struggling violently with this party. As it had been ascertained that six prisoners had been captured unwounded, and as it was three minutes to the signal for recall, Lieut.WOODMAN gave the return signal on the French Horn and attempted to get the wounded Boche over the top into No Man's Land. The wounded German struggled violently and resisted and eventually had to be shot. Lieut.WOODMAN and Lieut.WHITE returned with their parties to the British lines.

(2)

In the meantime Lieut. GOBLE had on entering the trenches at the appointed place turned to the left and at the head of his party proceeded down the trench towards point B. On passing through a bend in the trench near to where he entered Lieut. GOBLE saw three Germans running away down the trench. At the head of his men he pursued them, whereupon one of the Germans turned round and threw up his hands pleading for mercy. This man was taken prisoner and sent back, but in the meantime the two other Germans had managed to escape further up the trench and were pursued up to the entrance of a mine shaft. Lieut. GOBLE entered the shaft, but when approaching a chamber leading off to the right (similar to the one already spoken of) was fired on by at least three Germans with their rifles. He called to the Germans to surrender, in German, but they took no notice and proceeded to fire at the party with rifles and threw bombs whereupon the party replied with bombs and rifle fire and prepared to rush the dugout. At that time the signal for recall was heard from the top and Lieut. GOBLE after throwing all available bombs at the Germans re-entered the trench, crossed No Man's Land, and returned to the British trenches. The mine shaft appeared to be exactly similar to that described by Lieut. WOODMAN, in particular it had a similar steel covered piping.

The whole of the parties returned and were counted into the British trench. The Germans made no artillery retaliation whatever, but fired 3 rounds from trench mortars on "B" Company's lines by the SUNKEN road.

The prisoners were taken to the Headquarters of "D" Coy, thence the Battalion Headquarters, and eventually to Brigade Headquarters.

Communication was established from point W, and information was collected there by Lieut. S.P. DAVIES, being passed down by telephone to "D" Coy's Headquarters and thence to Battalion Headquarters.

The control of the Battalion front line trenches opposite the raided trench was under the direction of Lieut. R.G. STRUTT.

The Regimental Aid Post was established at P.73 under the direction of the Medical Officer.

The recall signals (2 bouquets of 6 red rockets)∅ were fired from the vicinity of D Company's Headquarters, and guiding Very Lights were sent up from PYLONES.

I have the honour to be

Sir,

Your obedient servant,

(Sgd) C.F.G. HOULDER.
Lieutenant-Colonel.
10/10/16.   Commanding 2/17th Battalion, London Regiment.

∅ Very lights were used, no rockets were fired.

TELEPHONE MESSAGES RECEIVED DURING THE RAID

of

2/17th London Regt.

- - - - - - - - - - - - - - - - -

1.50 a.m. First Shot fired.

1.55 a.m.   Party start to time and is now in Boche line. (3 mins. to get through on phone).

1.57 a.m.   Bombing in Boche line.

1.58 a.m.   Bringing three Boche over.
Another Boche. (Making four).
No retaliation.
No bombing in Boche trench.
Four Boche up to time.
More returning (referring to raid party).

2 a.m.   More men returning.
A whole crowd returning.

2.1 a.m.   The horn for returning is sounding, whole party coming back.

2.5 a.m.   No retaliation. Party has reach our line, the party is being counted.

2.6 a.m.   Whole party returned safely.
Hostile trench mortars open on "B" Coy.

2.7 a.m.   Regiment 104.

2.8 a.m.   Six Boche prisoners in all.

2.12 a.m.   Our artillery have finished. No casualties
            (Sting   reported yet. Artillery have ceased fire,
            (message.   but are standing by our targets. Everything
2.15 a.m.   quiet.

2.16 a.m.   The enemy have evidently returned behind DEVON.

2.25 a.m.   They think they killed four or five, full information not yet in.

2.40 a.m.   Boche passing Battalion H.Q. on way down.

2.42 a.m.   Three wounded, very slightly, but will not require to leave the trenches.

- - - - - - - - - -

60TH DIVISION

'A' & 'Q' BRANCH

~~JUN - NOV 1916~~

1914 DEC — 1915 MAR
1915 NOV — 1915 DEC
1916 MAY — 1916 NOV